THE LEADER'S BLUEPRINT
FOR CREATING A COMPELLING VISION
AND ENGAGING THE WORKFORCE

LEADING WITH VISION

BONNIE HAGEMANN
SIMON VETTER & JOHN MAKETA

"All leaders must read this book and, most importantly, put it to use immediately." **JIM KOUZES, co-author,** *The Leadership Challenge*

PRAISE FOR *LEADING WITH VISION*

"Enlisting others in a shared vision is the skill that most distinguishes leaders from individual contributors. It's also the most difficult to master, and as Bonnie Hagemann, Simon Vetter, and John Maketa make clear in *Leading with Vision*, it's the competency that's most lacking in the next generation of leaders. That's precisely why all leaders must read their new book and, most importantly, put it to use immediately. Backed by solid evidence, illustrated with compelling examples, and supported by practical applications, *Leading with Vision* is timely and essential reading. It will enable you to make the emotional connection that is absolutely necessary in engaging today's workforce."

—Jim Kouzes, coauthor, *The Leadership Challenge* and the Dean's Executive Fellow of Leadership, Leavey School of Business, Santa Clara University

"It's rare that a book combines genuine insights, practical advice, and compelling examples as superbly as Leading with Vision. Highly recommended as a guide for leaders seeking to inspire their organizations with a genuine, authentic vision."

—David B. Peterson, Ph.D., Director, Google's Center of Expertise, Leadership Development & Executive Coaching

"Regardless of level or title, this book is an essential guide for leaders who are committed to creating a new mindset at work, empowering their people and driving positive impact in their organizations."

—Randy Holloway, Director Cloud + Enterprise Solutions, Microsoft

"The perfect antidote for the current generational angst about Millennials. Through their research, the authors demonstrate that leadership can no longer be expressed through a 'father knows best' approach—proper leadership entails an engrossing corporate vision that motivates employees, elevates their work and encourages a bond with their organization. This is also what we need to keep bright young women from leaving corporate jobs in droves, especially in STEM areas. Timely and indispensable."

—Saniye Gülser Corat, Director, Division for Gender Equality, Office of Director-General, United Nations Educational, Scientific and Cultural Organization (UNESCO), France

"*Leading with Vision* shows leaders how to attain full engagement from the next generation of workers who are seeking an emotional connection to the work they do. And it tells the stories of many leaders who have successfully done so."

—Maureen McDonald, Former Vice President
Global Talent Management, Dell

"Leading is not easy in the best of times—and especially not in our current business environment, rife as it is with uncertainty, volatility and complexity. *Leading with Vision* is a lighthouse in that storm, filled with wise counsel for leaders who seek to engage and inspire their people."

—Marshall Goldsmith, executive coach and New
York Times-bestselling author, ranked the number one
leadership thinker in the world by Thinkers50

"*Leading with Vision* examines the challenges leaders face in engaging Millennials, which will be a majority of the workforce in 2025. The book highlights and discusses the importance of creating an emotional connection with this new workforce to get their full commitment, passion, and performance."

—Khaled El-Maleh, Ph.D., Senior Director of Technology, Qualcomm

"There is something here very much worth exploring . . . deeply. From the conceptual to current, real life business examples, to actionable questions and exercises, *Leading with Vision* takes readers on an authentic approach to focusing on the real driver of success—the factor behind the numbers—the corporation's people! Research and theory are matched with compelling business examples and actionable processes that will allow today's leader to focus on creating the connectedness that today and the future's workforce so crave. The business applications are real and the reading a joy as Hagemann et al seek to drag modern day leaders out of the fog in order to help create a workplace where today's generations are willing to take the stairs, two at a time!"

—Julie Laulis, CEO, Cable One, Inc.

"Creating a compelling vision that inspires people is not a simple task yet it is a powerful tool that impacts long term company performance. *Leading with Vision* provides a blueprint to help leaders create, articulate and deliver a compelling vision that will endure."

—Frances Hesselbein, CEO of The Frances Hesselbein Leadership Institute, named one of the World's 50 Greatest Leaders by Fortune

"A refreshing, evidence-based exploration into the power of a compelling vision—an often overlooked, but critical component of leading any organization!"

—Michael Traub, CEO Serta Simmons Bedding

"This book is a comprehensive guide for all leaders who want to improve their leadership capabilities towards becoming visionary leaders. It's essential for being and staying successful in an ever changing business world."

—Martin Knobloch, CEO Northern Europe BSH Home Appliances

"Creating a vision can be a highly inspiring and creative process within the company. This book shows how to achieve great results by involving employees in a bottom-up process without defining or even knowing the outcome."

—Stephan Haessig, Head High Networth Individual Clients UBS

"Reaching far beyond the recognition that today's leader needs to become the promoter of a meaningful and purpose-led culture, this 'change handbook' explains, through real-life examples, exactly how that can be achieved."

—Dr. Laurence S. Lyons, former Director of Research of the Future Work Forum at Henley Business School, co-author of *Creating Tomorrow's Organization*, and founding editor of *Coaching for Leadership*

"*Leading with Vision* can help you transform from being a leader who leads by numbers to one who truly leads by engaging employees with a clear, powerful, effective and inspiring vision, and then casting your employees as important players in that vision."

—Joel Garfinkle, author of Getting Ahead: Three
Steps to Take Your Career to the Next Level

"This a great book—essential to enterprise agility, as part of translating agile strategy and agile execution into traction, and avoiding wheel$pin."

—Mike Richardson, author, "Wheel$pin:
The Agile Executive's Manifesto"

"It's not enough to run a profitable business anymore. If you want to have your company matter, attract top talent and be a player, you are going to need to ensure your organization is purpose-driven. *Leading with Vision* will show you how."

—Tara Uzra Dawood, President, LADIESFUND
& Educate a Girl - Pakistan

"The authors of *Leading with Vision* use their experience, research, and client case studies to explain why connecting on an emotional level is the key to engaging the workforce of the future. If you're looking for ideas on how to do that, this book will get you started.

—Scott Eblin, best-selling author, global speaker and executive coach

"Leading today's workforce requires more than strategy and goals and financial success. Today's leaders have to be visionary and they must inspire the workforce to engage around the vision. It is not easy connecting vision to strategy to execution of goals. Leading with Vision is exactly what is needed for this environment. This book gives us both the why and the how of creating a compelling vision. It's a must read for leaders!"

—Tom Edwards, VP and GM Air Systems, Johnson Controls

LEADING
WITH
VISION

By Bonnie Hagemann,
Simon Vetter, and John Maketa

NICHOLAS BREALEY
PUBLISHING

BOSTON · LONDON

First published in the USA and UK in 2017 by Nicholas Brealey Publishing.
First paperback edition in 2020

An Hachette UK company

The Library of Congress Control Number: 2016056210

Hardcover ISBN: 978-1-85788-681-8
Trade Paperback ISBN: 978-1-47369-606-8
U.S. eBook ISBN: 978-1-85788-984-0
U.K. eBook ISBN: 978-1-85788-686-3

Printed in the United States of America

23 22 21 20   1 2 3 4 5 6 7

Nicholas Brealey Publishing policy is to use papers that are natural, renewable, and
recyclable products and made from wood grown in sustainable forests. The logging
and manufacturing processes are expected to conform to the environmental regula-
tions of the country of origin.

Nicholas Brealey Publishing
Carmelite House
50 Victoria Embankment
London EC4Y 0DZ
Tel: 020 7122 6000

Nicholas Brealey Publishing
Hachette Book Group
Market Place Center, 53 State Street
Boston, MA 02109, USA
Tel: (617) 523 3801

www.nbuspublishing.com

Contents

Introduction:

The Tidal Wave. xiii

Why This Book? Why Now? . . . . *xvii*

CHAPTER 1

The Disconnect 1

Generation Y *1*

A Widening Gap *3*

Leading by the Numbers. *4*

Dilbert Clones. *6*

The Research. *7*

Fog Can Be Very Dangerous *8*

The Driver *11*

Casting the Vision. *12*

The Newbies *13*

Getting Off the Roller Coaster. *14*

CHAPTER 2

Taking the Stairs Two at a Time 17

The Fuse. *18*

Why We All Need Apricot Pie. *19*

The Recipe for Success *19*

Seeing Is Believing. *21*

Belief Leads to Commitment. *22*

A New Mind-set at Work *22*

Safety First *27*

Takeaways from Chapter 2. . . . . *29*

CHAPTER 3

Who Gets Connectedness Right?. 31

Brand Initiative. 32

Culture: The Brand's Foundation. 33

Paying Attention 34

Leadership that Empowers 35

A Visionary Leader 37

The Soccer-playing CEO and the Turnaround 39

Competitive Challenge 40

Team Building 41

Bumble Bee Brand. 42

Visualizing Success 43

The Brand and the Vision. 44

Takeaways from Chapter 3 46

CHAPTER 4

Visionary Leadership at Work. 47

Embody Courage. 51

Forge Clarity. 54

Build Connectivity. 56

Shape Culture. 58

Takeaways from Chapter 4 61

CHAPTER 5

Embody Courage. 63

The Courage to be Bold 63

Better, Faster Customer Service—In Real Time. 64

Crowdsource Customer Service. 66

Convincing a Large Company to Adopt a New Business Model 67

A Bold Start 70

Game Changer 72

Organic Fruit in the Recycled Lunch Bag 72

The Courage to Be Vulnerable. 75

A Vision for Safety and a Dance *76*
Takeaways from Chapter 5 . . . . *82*

CHAPTER 6
Forge Clarity **83**

Three Levels of Clarity *85*
Create Accountability for Results and Behaviors *87*
Apply the Concept of Followership *88*
Team Charter, the "Secret" Weapon *89*
The March to Bodega Bay *91*
Clarity Before Strategy *92*
Clarity Is a Tool *95*
The Clarity of Conversation *97*
Takeaways from Chapter 6 . . . . *99*

CHAPTER 7
Build Connectivity **101**

The OluKai Story *103*
Ensuring Connectedness to the Brand *105*
Promoting the Spirit of Ohana *107*
Combining Private Equity Values with Family Values *110*
Creating an Office that Feels like Home *112*
A Culture of Connectedness *113*
The Process for Creating a Compelling Vision *114*
Takeaways from Chapter 7 . . . . *116*

CHAPTER 8
Shape Culture **119**

Culture at the Center of a Global Company: Hilti Corporation . . . *120*
Front and Center: Culture and Innovation *121*
Nuts and Bolts: The Process of Developing a Culture *122*
Testing and Implementing a Corporate Vision *123*

Building Innovation into the Culture *125*
Adjusting Processes and Encouraging Employee Flexibility *126*
Culture Planning Puts Hilti at the Top, Globally *127*
Quantifying Investment in Culture *128*
Leadership Development and Retention *129*
Hilti's Culture Planning Advice *130*
The Value of Culture Planning *132*
Takeaways from Chapter 8 . . . . *133*

CHAPTER 9
Obstacles to Leading with Vision **135**
Major Obstacle #1: Lack of Unity *135*
Major Obstacle #2: Preconceived Notions *139*
Major Obstacle #3: Lack of Buy-In Through the Organization *140*
Major Obstacle #4: A Lack of Urgency *147*
Major Obstacle #5: A Lack of Personal Development by the
Leader *148*
When a Strength Becomes a Liability *153*
Takeaways from Chapter 9 . . . . *154*

CHAPTER 10
Professor or Poet? **157**
Connecting with Emotions *157*
The Professor Turned Poet *159*
Painting the Picture *161*
Say It like You Mean It, like Your Life Depends on It *163*
Aristotle: The Poetics *164*
Becoming a Poet *165*
Takeaways from Chapter 10 . . . . *167*

CHAPTER 11
Storytelling **169**
Those Who Move Us *171*

Storytelling at Work: What It Means and Why It Matters 172
Leading People the Right Way 173
Doing the Right Things Right 174
Balancing Transactional and Transformational Leadership
Through Storytelling 174
Transmedia Storytellers 175
Succeeding as a Storyteller 178
Takeaways from Chapter 11 179

CHAPTER 12

A Blueprint to Creating a Compelling Vision 181
1. Imagine the Invisible 182
2. Vet the Vision 183
3. Create Options 184
4. Decide for Change 185
5. Communicate Effectively 188
6. Foster Understanding 189
Implementing the Fundamentals 189
Get Some Support 192
Takeaways from Chapter 12 193

CHAPTER 13

Conclusion 195

References 201
Index 211
About the Authors 220

Introduction:
The Tidal Wave

WHILE WALKING ALONG THE BEACH in San Diego in 2010, I was reflecting on the financial crisis of 2008 and its fallout, the changing workforce demographics, and the many components causing *the way we work* and *the way we view work* to shift. As I watched the water roll from small swells to towering waves along the shore, I thought about the powerful undertows beneath the surface—not obviously seen but capable of having immense impact on anyone caught in them. The scene was a good analogy for what was happening in business. The business world was also in a constant state of flux, morphing from one moment to another. Ever-changing expectations and external economic factors constantly shifted the playing field, with threats to business lurking beneath the surface along with new opportunities waiting to be uncovered. As I continued my walk, I thought about how dealing with this constant state of flux and shifting tide of competition requires effective leadership; it requires talented, resilient people, motivated and engaged at the highest level possible.

As the CEO of Executive Development Associates (EDA), I lead an organization that has, for 34 years, developed leaders at the top-of-the-house across every industry around the world. Along with my coauthors, John Maketa and Simon Vetter, I am on the front lines of the challenges businesses across the world are facing. This book is designed to share insights into some of the biggest transformational shifts happening in businesses today.

This work began when Simon, John, and I were in a conference room in San Diego—Simon's base city—to discuss the results of EDA's biennial *Trends in Executive Development* survey, which was pointing to a significant need identified by respondents: *leaders who can create a compelling vision and engage others around it.* According to the 466 companies who participated in the research, that need was both a top priority AND also perceived as the most lacking competency in next-generation leaders. Accordingly, we have developed a framework and an actionable blueprint to help leaders navigate their companies to a successful future through what we now refer to as *leading with vision.* Collectively, the three of us have worked across almost every industry and with a great many leaders. We have observed the full range of leadership theories along with what actually happens in practice—"at the sharp end," as they say. We stay close to both the work and the research in order to have our fingers on the pulse of what is really happening in the business world. We then use what we find to help leaders to implement strategies and make the best decisions for their organizations.

At our meeting in San Diego, we discussed how things were shifting in a very significant and very interesting way. In fact, it seemed to us that the blue ocean of business was now resembling a tidal wave, with profound and far-reaching consequences driven powerfully by the undertow of technology combined with demographic shifts. These shifts are just beginning to gain momentum and will continue to impact all businesses everywhere.

One major shift in recent years is that leaders are currently dealing with a very different group of people entering the workplace. The Boomer generation of the post-war years (over 77 million workers in the United States alone)—largely motivated by hard work, loyalty, financial gain, and job security—are retiring and leaving the workforce at a rate of 10,000 per day. For a time, Generation X had moved into the workforce with a fairly low impact, assimilating into the Boomer workplace, but now everything is changing. A new workforce is emerging—Generation Y—and they are massive, already outnumbering Gen X in the workplace and working their way to becoming 75 percent of the workforce by 2025. Most important, they are a whole new story. Today's corporate leaders simply don't understand how to lead them and how to motivate them. And that is a problem.

Creating a compelling vision and engaging teams to deliver the vision have always been key aspects of effective leadership that have been documented in almost every business book for the past 30 years or more. The issue now is that leaders are finding that what motivated previous generations doesn't compel Gen Y. In fact, this extremely creative and talented bunch are either never entering the workforce or are leaving in droves, and leaders are scrambling to figure out how to stop the exodus. Where are they going? Your first thought may be that they are going to their parents' basement. That may be true, but don't judge them yet—they may be creating the next Facebook or Airbnb from that basement. But corporations need their talent too, and for leaders to engage today's—and tomorrow's—workforce, they will need to create an environment in which Gen Y will choose to participate.

The recession of 2008 and the years following caused leaders everywhere to focus on urgent financial needs, often at the cost of focusing on the important shifts caused by technology and demographics. The major storm diverted their attention from the changing tide, and as a result, many leaders in the business world have now been caught unprepared.

Before you decide whether or not *your* organization's leadership bench is sufficient, take a moment to assess your current senior leadership team to determine whether you have capable successors for all mission-critical positions. It is, of course, important to use the right criteria, such as what skills and experience successors will need to have in order to be effective leading your organization into the future. Potential successors must either possess or have the potential to gain the business and leadership skills required. Each organization has its business criteria, but leading with vision is a top-of-the-house need for all.

With that in mind, review each mission-critical position for the necessary skills including this attribute on your organizational chart one by one with each job title in the appropriate box. If you have someone who is ready now to take the role, make that box green. If you have someone who will be ready in the next two or three years, make that box yellow. If you do not have anyone in the pipeline who seems to be capable of filling that role, make that box red. This should paint a picture of whether or not your organization is prepared for the demographic shift that is a large contributor to the current leadership challenge and which we will discuss throughout the book. Employees and leaders are floundering, battered by waves of change and uncertainty with no rule book to guide them. Below is an example of one organization's chart upon completion of this exercise:

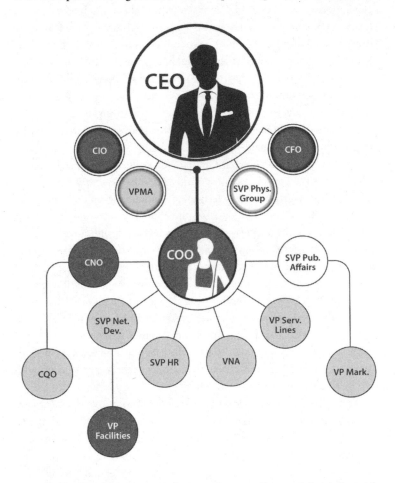

The dark circles are red, the light circles are yellow and the circles with the white in the middle are green. The more we researched the issue of how to create a compelling vision that would actually capture Generation Y, the more we realized that leaders need to make a crucial shift: they need to connect with their employees on an emotional rather than a cognitive level. We wanted to understand the issues ourselves, so in addition to our own research and experience, we set out to learn from many top leaders and drew on the most significant work in the field. It's been a great learning experience for us, and we hope that in the following pages you will find information that is helpful to you. Together we can learn from the research, our work at the sharp end, and from some of the leaders who have learned to lead with vision and engage others around it.

WHY THIS BOOK? WHY NOW?

Businesses are facing a ruthless, competitive climate, and to navigate a successful route through these volatile, uncertain, complex, and ambiguous times requires a new, more thoughtful, and relevant approach. The rapid changes will most likely accelerate. With this comes the need to constantly adjust course and adapt to be agile and purposeful and to engage and develop the talents of everyone in the business. The quantitative and qualitative research indicates that there is a better and much more effective way to do this going forward—one that will ensure higher returns for organizations in talent, innovation, and competitiveness and that is connecting the heart of your people to the vision or mission of the organization and ensuring that they understand their role and feel a part of bringing it to reality.

This book introduces a new way of thinking about leading the workforce. Our approach recognizes the need to lead people with vision, to explain what it means in practice to display visionary leadership, to show who does it well, and to highlight the results that can be achieved. And while we recognize that it is the younger generation that is forcing change, we should make it clear that everything we discuss in the book is relevant to all employees, at whatever age, because we all want to feel connected to something and be valued as a contributor.

Vision, visionary leadership, and *engagement* are terms that are often used but only rarely understood or applied consistently. This book explains what it means—in practice—to lead, inspire, and engage people with a vision and purpose, and it explores the qualities needed to succeed. To lead with vision, leaders must display courage, provide clarity, shape and enhance the culture, and energize and connect with people at all levels, both inside and outside the company. Some of the best, most inspiring, and effective businesses and brands of the last decade share the ability to do this incredibly well.

Before we continue, now is a good place to formally introduce myself (your narrator) and my coauthors, whose stories and examples will be shared here along with my own.

I grew up in the Midwest and came to the corporate world with a roll-up-my-sleeves-and-get-to-work attitude. Those same Midwestern roots drive me to search for the most meaningful and authentic aspects of business. However, as much as I'm driven to tackle an unending string of new challenges with the most interesting and powerful corporate leaders, my favorite place on earth is still the swing on my back porch. And my favorite leaders to coach are those not-yet-fully-formed teenagers across my kitchen table—they are, after all, our future.

Simon, a San Diego local, is a charismatic, passionate, and thought-provoking Swiss who speaks, coaches, and writes about leadership. He is well known and highly regarded for his work helping leaders stand out, and he is the anchor in our group; his thoughtful Swiss nature is the perfect counterpoint for our Western bravado. His careful disposition has proven helpful in the pages to come, because without his insistence on having more discussions and mining more analysis and data, we would never have captured such a complete picture.

John is a gregarious, anything-can-be-accomplished influencer from Philadelphia. He has a long history in leadership development and works in the talent assessment and human capital space. He loves to make deals, but what drives him more than making money in the corporate world is his desire to inspire others. He is the type of guy who would have Richard Branson's top ten inspirational quotes covering the walls of his home office. I can't remember a single time when he failed to convince an entire room of whatever point he was driving that day. He passionately debates key points, drawing on a wealth of commercial experience, and drops logic bombs into the middle of our many academic discussions.

Because our work is based on research, we wanted to ensure that we shared what we learned in an engaging way versus a typical academic text. So, we decided to utilize one of the powerful concepts often used by people who do well at leading with vision, and that is conveying the message primarily through storytelling. The book itself is the story of our journey to uncover the power and the how-to of a compelling vision, and we have also included powerful stories about companies who do it well. Thus, we hope it feels more like we are sitting around the kitchen table together than sitting in a classroom. Since a cornerstone of our framework is connectedness, what better way to connect than by sharing the story of what we learned as we explored what really compels people to follow a leader, connect to an organization, and engage around a shared vision?

CHAPTER 1

The Disconnect

L ET'S RETURN TO THAT CONFERENCE ROOM in San Diego where Simon, John, and I started to think about how we could find ways to help leaders create a compelling vision and engage others around it, particularly the Gen Y members who almost demand to be motivated and inspired before they will opt in. In addition to what we'd seen in our field work, we were very focused on the research, which clearly indicated that the trends in executive development were shifting and that leading with vision and employee engagement were now the key indicators for success. The first thing we wanted to do was compare notes about what we'd seen in the workplace, so we shared some anecdotes and insights.

GENERATION Y

Generation Y was born in the 1980s and 1990s. Most are children of the Boomers; they are typically perceived as being increasingly familiar with digital and electronic technology, and they are credited with actively shaping today's corporate culture and employee expectations.

Simon began by telling us a story about Bruce, the Gen Y son of his friend Mike. Bruce is a twenty-five-year-old graduate with a degree in accounting and finance. Right out of university, he went to work for a renowned Fortune500 company. Initially, he was extremely excited. It was a huge company with a great brand and a great reputation, but after only a few months Bruce went to his father and said, "Dad, I'm out. This place sucks."

Taken aback, Mike asked what had happened. Bruce said, "I work in a cubicle. Every morning my manager walks by my cubicle. He walks by again every day at lunch. He walks by in the afternoon. And then, he walks by at the end of each day. He never even looks at me when he passes my cubicle."

Mike saw the picture but hoped Bruce wasn't jumping too soon. He said, "Maybe you should give it a few more weeks. The manager might change, or you might get a new manager."

"No, I'm done. I'm out," Bruce said.

Bruce quit and started looking for another job. A few months later, he got a position with a start-up, a small email security company. His role moved slightly from straight finance to a more sales-support finance role. His clients were on the East Coast, and he was on the West coast, meaning the clients started their workday at 5:00 A.M. Pacific time. Using his flex time, Bruce shifted his hours to accommodate his clients. Now, he gets to work at 5:00 A.M. every morning. He's the first person in the office. At 6:00 A.M. the CEO arrives. He always walks by Bruce's office, peeks in, and checks with him. Even when Bruce is on the phone, the CEO gives him a thumbs-up through the open door, just recognizing that he's there, which clearly lets him know he's important. Bruce loves his new job, and, to top it off, he gets paid more and has stock options.

This anecdote sums it all up: Truly engaging your people is paramount. It makes all the difference to your success as an organization. Every employee, no matter what generation they are, wants to feel engaged with their work and understand what they are helping to achieve. However, the Boomers and Gen Xers may be content to clock-in and clock-out, wishing away the hours and/or doing the bare minimum, but Generation Y is built differently. They want to be engaged, stimulated, motivated, and involved. If they aren't, then they leave.

As Bruce's reaction illustrates, big companies with great names can no longer rely on their reputation to attract and retain their talent pool. Instead, they need a compelling vision and a way to create personal connectedness. Otherwise, employees won't commit to the organization.

The research we will share in chapter 4 shows that creating this personal connectedness will achieve increased organizational commitment, lower staff turnover, and produce higher returns to the bottom line. In Bruce's case, if he had been personally connected to the company's vision, he may have decided to stay there rather than move to another company, despite its lackluster manager. Connectedness would also have helped the company keep a talented person who was willing to go above and beyond and who was prepared to come into work at 5:00 A.M. every day to help clients across the continent. Losing Bruce was a serious loss for that company.

A WIDENING GAP

John had a disengaging experience from his own work past to share. For one of his past employers, he attended a strategy session with his manager and ten colleagues to review plans for the next year. They met in a drab hotel conference room with only one window, and the blinds were half drawn. Here's how John described the day. "It was foggy outside, and when my manager shared her Excel spreadsheet with the team, my brain became even foggier. We went through it line by excruciating line—all day, trying to determine which products were making the most profit, what the margins were, where expenses could be lowered, which markets we should focus on, and the price of eggs in China. . .

Here's the truth: It's not all about the money. People may leave for money, but they'll stay in spite of the money if they're personally connected to the organization—that is, if they feel confident, excited, and even inspired.

"We hovered over and around that damn spreadsheet for hours. By the end of the day, we were all beyond exhausted. The only thing we were looking forward to was drinks. Afterward, we made our way to the bar, where we ordered pitchers of margaritas, asked the bartender to turn on *Survivor*, and then worked really hard to forget about the business for a while. My only connection to the company that day was my fellow drinking buddies and the happy hour mental escape.

"The very next day, I was eating lunch at my desk when a recruiter called. He said, 'I have a great opportunity to talk to you about.' I looked through my office window, remembered the previous day's meeting, turned my chair around, and said, 'I'm so glad you called. Whaddya got?' I couldn't wait to get out of there." Motivation is everything.

LEADING BY THE NUMBERS

The scene that John wanted to escape is all too common. In our experience across industries and continents, we've found that leaders are more likely to lead with numbers than vision. Leaders of public companies are often the most likely to use the spreadsheet approach, perhaps because they are rewarded almost solely on data-driven shareholder value. How do leaders determine shareholder value? Through a series of financial spreadsheets. But, is that enough?

The shareholders aren't asking, "Are your employees connected to the organization?" or, "Do they feel important at work?" No; shareholders are asking, "Where's my return on investment?" Public-company leaders—and leaders in many other organizations—are conditioned to focus on numbers instead of people, but here's the issue: *people drive the numbers*. Numbers may be inspiring for the sales team or for the senior leaders whose bonuses are impacted, but the majority of employees are not compelled to go to work every day to help the company hit a number. A number is not a vision.

In fact, sometimes even a cool environment, high salaries, and great benefits aren't enough to effectively support and retain employees, and companies need to take the time to figure out if there's another problem or if another key piece is missing. For instance, I did some work in an organization with a surprising situation. It is a huge, multibillion-dollar corporation, a top competitor in its field. It was one of the coolest and hippest environments imaginable. The facilities were incredible, the benefits were over the top, and the employees were paid generous salaries. The organization had gyms, restaurants, and even an employee garden. It gave out sports team tickets to employees. The workforce was fairly young and energetic. Everyone wanted to work there.

Until they did.

Once they were employed, the trade-off became clear. It was an extreme work environment, with long hours and weekend work expected at every level. Many employees who worked there began to suffer myriad health issues—often related to stress and anxiety. They were burned out, depressed, and so anxious that they started missing work to attend doctors' appointments to get antidepressants and antianxiety medications. Over time, the loss of hours on the job started to impact the bottom line, and the company's leaders knew something had to be done.

You may think that the leaders tried to get to the bottom of their employees' discontent or that they researched what it could possibly be in such a stunning environment with high salaries that depressed their employees. You may think that they were going to make changes to the working conditions that were making people sick. But, no. That's not what happened. Instead, they just streamlined the process of getting their employees' prescriptions refilled: they hired an on-site physician.

Problem solved? You guessed it: not by a long shot.

In 1954, Abraham Maslow presented his theory that once our basic needs of food, health, and housing have been met, we all then strive for love and belonging (McLeod 2013). We want to be part of a community. We seek inclusion. After that, we want respect, because self-esteem is important to our mental well-being. As long as people have enough money to cover their bills, they are more likely to stay with a company that offers them a sense of connectedness and shows them respect than they are to chase more dollars with an organization that doesn't address these higher-level but still fundamental needs.

DILBERT CLONES

Organizations of all sizes grapple with employee disengagement. Consider one of John's past clients, a large conglomerate with over 36,000 employees. In his work, he found that there was an entire department where the employees from the front line to the vice president had no idea what they were supposed to be doing. The organization had been through a massive reorganization to operate as a matrix, and in the process chaos took over. A matrix organizational structure is one where there are shared services across departments. For example, marketing may be a shared service. So there is one marketing department and it serves all of the business units. The same is often true for accounting, engineering, sales, project management, etc. Then there are business unit leaders who are responsible for overseeing products and services. This type of structure often requires dual reporting lines, as an engineer may technically work for the VP over engineering (hard line) but will have a dual reporting relationship (dotted line) to the business unit leader where the work is being conducted.

The employees in this particular department wanted to do a good job, but they would start working on a project only to see it scrapped or the direction changed. They were frustrated and bored. They weren't challenged or stimulated, and they openly shared that morale was extremely low in the department. The reorganization lasted a long time—too long—and in the process, the best talent in this department left. They were unwilling to wait until the organization was reset in order to add value. They lost their connection and many felt they didn't have a reason to stay.

Without a sense of connectedness, people can begin to do strange things, including giving up big salaries or leaving without confirmed employment elsewhere. While many employees do their best to be productive, regardless of whether or not they feel connected to the organization or its vision, others begin to take on the characteristics of the cartoon character Dilbert, spending as much time trying to avoid meaningful work as they do trying to produce it. The work, for them, becomes a daily grind where they force themselves up the stairs on the way to work—and then take those exact same stairs two at a time on the way out in the evening.

The goal of creating a compelling vision is to reverse this scenario so that employees start the working day excited, taking the stairs two steps at a time and giving 100 percent effort while at work. They are energized and excited by the opportunity to be an important and valued part of the story.

THE RESEARCH

As mentioned in the introduction, our *Trends in Executive Development* (Hagemann et al., 2016) research revealed that the ability to create a compelling vision and engage others around it has become the number one challenge in leadership competency development and is essential for executives to develop if they are to inspire others, command loyalty, and keep talent engaged. It is also the most lacking leadership competency in next-generation leaders. As we noted in our *Trends* report, "As we look at the future we see an ever-more, hyper-competitive business environment, where the most successful organizations will be the ones with leaders who can create a compelling vision—and who can convey that vision to customers and employees."

The *Trends in Executive Development* survey has been conducted by Executive Development Associates, Inc.[1] approximately every two years since the early 1980s, and 2016 was the first time that creating a compelling vision and engaging others around it had been the number one trend. Once this competency rose to the top, John, Simon, and I went to work to understand it further. What we learned is that creating a vision is difficult for most leaders, and creating a *compelling* vision is profoundly difficult for almost all of them.

If we are to get technical about it, a vision has to be visual; that is to say, it needs to be something people can see in their mind's eye. However, to be compelling, there has to be more to it than that. Employees can be very clear about the vision and have the picture firmly in their mind

---

[1] For further information see Executive Development Associates website, *www .executivedevelopment.com.*

without having it in their heart. They could show up for work every day and still not be connected to the organization or to the vision. For it to be compelling, employees have to believe in it. They have to desire it. They have to *feel* connected to the vision in a very personal way.

But what are the key ingredients that make a vision really compelling? What is needed for employees to feel it and to get excited? Therein lies the crux of the problem.

FOG CAN BE VERY DANGEROUS

Let's look at why creating a vision that is clear can be a difficult challenge. Many organizations have visions that do not mean anything. A few years ago, Simon met with Stan, the vice president of sales in a large software company. Simon asked, "What is the vision for your company?"

Stan gave Simon a blank look, reached into his drawer, and then pulled out a three-by-five-inch index card. He started reciting the words printed on the card. His voice was dry and monotone, as if he were reading a legal document, and his face revealed no enthusiasm whatsoever. Who could blame him? The words he read were downright *boring*. Stan wasn't engaged around the vision. He was reading it, but he wasn't compelled, and he wasn't seeing it. He was in the fog that so many leaders and employees are in when it comes to vision. Here's a visualization to make the point.

A few years ago Simon and four friends went skiing in Davos, Switzerland. One afternoon, they took a six-mile downhill run from the top of the mountain down into the village. Clouds moved in quickly, turning into thick fog with a heavy snowstorm and winds. Since there were no trees around, it was really hard to see the slope path. They couldn't see farther than twenty yards; they lost orientation, and almost lost themselves in the fog. Consequently they moved slowly and cautiously to navigate downhill. It was really dangerous and scary because there was no vision.

The next day, Simon and his friends got up early and were back at the same mountaintop with different conditions. The sun was shining bright over the mountain peaks. There was blue sky and two feet of fresh powder. When they stood on the top of the mountain, the panorama was breathtaking and the excitement high. As they took turns in the deep powder and let the fresh snow splash into their faces, they yelled out of joy and gave each other high fives after each run. It was a once-in-a-lifetime ski event.

Relating this concept of fog and vision to business, here are two questions to ponder. Which situation do you experience in your organization?

1. Is your company operating in the fog, getting disoriented, uncertain, or even lost in the minutiae, managers and employees being fearful of making a decision, or feeling nervous and scared of taking action?

2. Or does your company have a compelling vision with a clear sense of direction; a well-defined path for the future; people being courageous and decisive, taking initiative and calculated risk, enthusiastic and joyful to be part of an exciting journey?

Many organizational leaders and employees are trying to see and maneuver themselves through the fog. The fog for leaders is our current VUCA environment, a term that we've adopted from an acronym that emerged from the military in the 1990s. It stands for Volatile, Uncertain, Complex, and Ambiguous, and it describes the "fog of war"—the chaotic conditions of a modern battlefield. These conditions are also highly descriptive of the environment in which business is conducted every day; however, the fog for leaders is brought on by the influx of disruptive ideas, technology culture shock, shifting demographics, customer evolution, and global financial turmoil. Leadership as usual—including creating a vision—is not enough in a VUCA world. The path isn't clear; the fog is thick, and leaders can't see very far ahead. So they feel cautious and afraid of making quick, bold decisions, and they avoid risk. Instead of seeing the opportunities, they see the obstacles.

The lesson is clear. Leaders in a fog are so focused on the immediate road ahead—the problems, quotas, quarterly profits, stock price, and all the other key performance indicators—that they focus on the short term and lose the view of the long term. Is it any wonder that they have trouble leading with vision?

Without a strong vision and sense of direction to guide them, leaders become nearsighted, overly cautious, uninspired, and uninspiring. Over time, this inevitably and dramatically compromises an organization's speed, agility, and progress. This is the true danger of being lost in a fog.

On the other hand, when leaders share a clear, sharp, compelling vision of the future, employees get excited. They become innovative and committed. They plan ahead, set ambitious targets, and take inspired action. That's the power of vision unleashed.

When Vision Works

Many companies have vision statements but, frankly, most of them are not very powerful. They are like plain vanilla and not at all inspiring. They offer no personal connection. Of course, that's not always the case—some companies have created very powerful visions and then made them into a reality. Let's look at some memorable vision statements that have worked well.

Microsoft: A COMPUTER ON EVERY DESK

In the late 1970s, Microsoft had a compelling vision: "A computer on every desk, and in every home, running Microsoft software." That was a crystal-clear vision of the future—one that any employee could feel part of. It was unique, and the goal was big and audacious. It was compelling. And, in spite of serious competition, Microsoft has experienced great success at reaching this goal. (Even now I'm writing this on my Microsoft Surface Pro.)

Kodak: A CAMERA AS CONVENIENT AS THE PENCIL

Then there was George Eastman's vision for Kodak in the early 1900s: "To make the camera as convenient as the pencil." In the early 1990s Kodak went into a long season of financial struggles, but its initial vision by Eastman was crystal clear and compelling. It was a positive, future-orientated statement to which everyone could feel connected. The employees could imagine themselves working toward this one unified vision. They knew, even then, that they were part of something that was going to touch many, many people for a long time.

THE DRIVER

The vision for the organization is like the driver in a car. If the driver is going to take you somewhere, you have to know where you want to go and give them an address. The driver then knows where to go and gets you there.

Whenever I'm in the Washington, D.C., area, I know I can rely on a driver named Gupta. I always let him know when I'll arrive at Baltimore Washington International Airport, and he waits for me in the designated passenger pickup location. While I'm clear about where I want to go, he's the one who makes sure I arrive there. He also makes sure that I feel important to him along the way—that I'm a part of the journey and so is he. For instance, he remembers our conversations from past drives, and he remembers what kind of charger I need for my phone. He hands me water, and he doesn't take distracting calls while we travel together. In these ways, Gupta is a savvy businessman. By making a personal connection with me, he's won my loyalty.

*"Would you tell me, please, which way
I ought to go from here?"*

*"That depends a good deal on where you
want to get to."*

"I don't much care where—"

"Then it doesn't matter which way you go."

—Lewis Carroll, *Alice in Wonderland*

Leaders need to take the same approach as Gupta and make sure they connect the people with the organization and its vision. Smart leaders have known for a long time that business is about relationships. However, the focus has always been on the relationship with the customer (and maybe the supplier), often neglecting the employee.

CASTING THE VISION

I asked the president of a $250 million manufacturing company, "What's the vision?"

"Five hundred million dollars in five years," he answered.

On another occasion, I asked the CEO of a multibillion-dollar energy business, "What's the vision?"

"Grow the business by thirty percent in the next three years," he said.

I asked another CEO of a multibillion-dollar mining business, "What's the vision?"

He answered, "Standard EBITA and increasing shareholder value."

Of course, these were not the corporate vision statements that they probably had printed on index cards, but this is what rolled off the top executives' tongues when I asked the question "What is your vision." It's hardly surprising that financial results were uppermost in their thinking, but it takes us back to our earlier point that a number is not a vision.

We're not trying to be flippant on this point. We know that it's hard to create a compelling vision and that going beyond the numbers can be difficult for leaders, especially when their rewards directly depend on those numbers. But the fact that it's hard doesn't mean it isn't worth the effort. The environment is shifting, and a new focus on vision is essential. If leaders can learn anything from Microsoft and Kodak, it is that their visions had a purpose that was more than just about numbers. They created an exciting aspiration that people could buy in to.

THE NEWBIES

As noted earlier, the necessity to lead with vision comes from the new generation of employees. They're the ones who are currently creating one of the biggest shifts in the workforce. The problem is that leaders are still treating them like they treated the last generation—and this simply isn't working. The newbies are either not joining the corporate world at all or choosing to leave it in droves. Like Bruce, who left a big brand for a smaller company, they are simply not willing to spend the currency of their lives in an environment where they're not valued and where they feel no meaning in the work they do.

These brilliant young minds won't be moved by facts and figures. They need an emotional stake in the game.

The reality is that many young people would rather go home, live in their parents' garage, get a job at Starbucks, and get creative trying to build the next big thing. That isn't a joke or a dig at Gen Y. That's what they're doing. This generation has needs that must be met if you expect them to use their time on a job. And what are those needs?

First and foremost, for them to become truly engaged in the vision, Gen Y needs to feel that what they're doing has some sort of positive social impact. The older generations need to adapt to the new parameters of what employees expect from their careers. Leaders can't just ignore what three quarters of the workforce are expecting and demanding.

Gen Y isn't interested in spreadsheets, because they don't believe that a company is a group of numbers. They believe that a company is a group of people with a story to tell. You can't woo them with numbers, but you can win them by offering them an important part in the story. They don't want dry facts. They want the romance and excitement of something bigger than themselves. Without this inspiration, you'll leave them thinking, "How about a tall mocha latte instead? It sounds infinitely more appealing." And that's what you, as a leader, have to compete with in your search for talent.

GETTING OFF THE ROLLER COASTER

During our San Diego meeting, John shared a final anecdote about a neighbor. Initially, he was a happy, gregarious fellow—funny and fun to be around. However, he spent several years of his life in a very well-known global telecommunications company with an unhealthy culture. This particular company offered their employees a frightening roller coaster ride of layoffs and rehires—over and over again. That depressing set of circumstances made the employees feel undervalued and vulnerable. Their only real connection in this business maelstrom was the hope of getting rehired. The best they could hope for was to hear, "See, you're one of the lucky ones; the company wants to hire you back, so we must like you."

This approach is hardly convincing, and it certainly is not motivating. Instead, it is more likely to engender fear and entrenchment than to energize and motivate people to seek new ways to help grow the business. John's neighbor went through multiple rounds of this layoff-rehire scenario during his time with the company.

Imagine someone getting on a terrifying roller coaster ride with brown hair and getting off with gray hair. People often age quickly under deep stress. Just review the physical appearance change in your president or prime minister during their tenure. While John's neighbor's hair didn't turn gray, his health undeniably suffered from the stress of losing his job so many times. He lost his sense of fun, along with his sunny personality, and he gained a lot of weight. Finally, after fifteen years of this, when the company called to rehire him for the seventh time, he refused to go back. Instead, he took a severance package and went back to school to become a nurse—a career with a clear vision, a meaningful mission, and one to which he felt connected.

Here's the point. Staying for fifteen years in an unhealthy environment is what the older generations have been willing to do. This new generation? Maybe they'll stay fifteen minutes. It's just not going to happen. This generation, the one our future business success relies on, needs something more.

Unfortunately, leaders aren't equipped to provide an effective and compelling vision for this emerging workforce because they either don't know how or they fundamentally don't recognize that Gen Y has different needs and that they are actively changing the rules of engagement. They need an emotional stake in the game.

Leaders urgently need to address this shortfall. There's a powerful tidal wave coming to corporations worldwide. It doesn't respect the numbers. It doesn't respect the past. Leaders can't pretend this change doesn't exist or try to cast the new generation into an old mold. They have to motivate and engage people on these new terms, which is the only way to get the most from people and unleash all their talent and creativity.

CHAPTER 2

Taking the Stairs Two at a Time

I N 2006 I HAD A MEETING WITH JIM BOLT, the founder of Executive Development Associates (EDA), to discuss how I would run the company. Jim had been developing senior leaders since the early 1980s and was a renowned expert in the field. I knew I had much to learn from Jim and hoped we could work together. I didn't know at the time that the very first piece of advice he would give me would shape and inform every leadership decision I have made since. And, much like the advice my colleagues and I are trying to impart now, it came from a book.

We met at Jim's home in San Diego, which he had designed himself. After a few pleasantries and a tour, we walked through his living room, went out the back door, and crossed the canopied courtyard to his unattached home office.

We brainstormed for a while, batting ideas and back and forth, and it was clear that we were both excited about where the company could go. We were both making notes and looking for points of common ground and vision for the future. Eventually, we concluded that we would be able to put something together. Then, we began to talk casually, perusing his books and getting to know each other.

Jim pulled a book from the shelf called *Let My People Go Surfing* by Yvon Chouinard, founder and CEO of Patagonia, a sports clothing company. He handed it to me with enthusiasm.

"If we get this thing going, we should do this," he said.

"Do what?" I asked.

"One percent for the planet. They talk about it in this book."

I couldn't wait to get home and begin reading, and I wasn't disappointed. The point Jim was referring to was a mission for organizations to give 1 percent of their profit to help the planet. Now, as much as I am a firm believer in giving back to the planet, it was something else within the pages that captivated me. The CEO of Patagonia wanted to build an organization where employees were compelled to come to work. Patagonia is more than a company. It's an environmental mission initially inspired by Yvon Chouinard's ambitious climbing expeditions. For employees to be a part of that mission, he noted, "Work had to be enjoyable on a daily basis. We all had to come to work on the balls of our feet and go up the stairs two steps at a time" (Chouinard 2005, 45).

THE FUSE

Imagine, employees taking the stairs two steps at a time on the way to work. Whether he intended to or not, Jim had lit a fuse. I needed to know more. The book was incredibly inspiring as it described the mission and the people who made the story of Patagonia come to life. The story centers around their private journey and their effort to get clear on what compelled them. Ultimately, they had created something that worked for them. They had the magic that connected their employees to the story of Patagonia.

Of course, I knew that every company couldn't be like that one, but I wondered if every company could create some of their own magic. Could every company build a vision, mission, or purpose that was different, unique, and important and that created an atmosphere that was compelling? The more I thought about it, the more essential it seemed.

I shared this story with John and Simon, and we asked ourselves, "Have we ever worked for a company where we wanted to take the stairs two steps at a time?" Simon told us that the Patagonia story reminded him of when he was a boy in Bern, Switzerland.

Simon's memory wasn't about working for a company, but he related a vivid picture of taking the stairs two steps at a time. He was around twelve years old, and after school he often played soccer with his friends. But on Wednesdays at 6:00 P.M., regardless of how exciting the game had become, he stopped playing and ran home, because on Wednesdays Simon's mom made apricot pie. Simon explained, "She made it fresh every Wednesday with a thin crust and lots of whipped cream and served it with ice cream."

WHY WE ALL NEED APRICOT PIE

Simon's mother's apricot pie was his favorite thing in the world after playing soccer, so he ran home. He sprinted across the field and down the hill and through the streets and finally up the stairs, two steps at a time. He was so excited. He was hungry, of course, but it was more than that. He would burst into the house and sit down at the kitchen table. Then his mom would proudly bring him a slice of hot pie, piled with whipped cream and ice cream on the side and served with very cold milk. He loved the pie, but he also knew that his mom baked it because she loved him, and it was one of the ways that she showed it. That made it even more compelling. And that experience, drive, and motivation is what a compelling vision is like.

Now, imagine an organization where people come to work in the morning and they don't just shuffle. They hurry, taking two steps at a time. They feel important. They're so excited to be a part of a big goal or to tackle a captivating project that they know will affect their future or the future of others in a positive way. Leaders need to create the apricot pie experience for their employees and give them a reason to get excited about the work. So, how can leaders create a compelling vision of a future state and then communicate it in a way that excites people, and how can doing the day-to-day work become compelling?

THE RECIPE FOR SUCCESS

I think we can all agree that if we take the time and effort to discover what it takes for our organizations to become so compelling that the employees take the stairs two steps at a time on the way to work, we will have something very powerful. Unquestionably, it will help leaders advance the strategy and grow their organizations.

With this in mind, my coauthors and I began to seek out the research and experiences that would aid us in this discovery process. We settled on several core issues early on, such as the definition of a vision, the scientific support for having a compelling vision, and the fact that most leaders really don't know how to be visionaries—perhaps because the majority of them run their companies by visualizing an uninspiring financial analysis rather than a compelling story.

For us, the definition of a vision is this: a clear picture of a positive future state. For organizations, a vision articulates this view of a realistic, desirable, and positive future state. It is designed to provide people with the compelling reason to make progress toward that state and accomplish the organization's goals. The vision answers, indirectly, the question of where the company is going.

There are two areas of scientific research that tie directly to the power of a compelling vision. The first is based on the concept of visualizing a positive future state, and the second is based on how that vision impacts people in the workplace. Much research has gone into the power of visualization. Even though many of us do not think of ourselves as using it personally as a tool, we do understand that many people, notably world-class professional athletes, use it as a method to mentally prepare for competition.

In fact, visualization as a technique was popularized by the Soviets in the 1970's for competing in sports (LeVan 2009). Today, "brain studies have revealed that thoughts produce the same mental instructions as actions. Mental imagery impacts many cognitive processes in the brain: motor control, attention, perception, planning, and memory. So the brain is getting trained for actual performance during visualization" (LeVan 2009).

When visualization is used in sports, an athlete visualizes the scene and the positive future state of that scene. We will explore visualization as a part of the process further in chapter 6 when we discuss clarity. During sports visualization the athlete is the main character, which makes the future state very compelling. This is an important point. How can leaders make the vision for their company resonate in a way that employees see themselves as a primary character in the story?

SEEING IS BELIEVING

Creating a compelling vision for a business is, in effect, a visualization exercise for the entire organization. Unfortunately, it isn't usually created or shared in a way in which employees feel that they are an important character in the story (Fallon Taylor 2015). See if this story sounds familiar: Employees come into an organization, sit through orientation, and receive their laminated index cards containing the company's vision mission, and values. Of course, they know that the goal of the cards is to define where the company is going, but the cards go directly into desk drawers, where they are quickly forgotten. In fact, the cards are still there when the employees leave months or years later. If the employees have revisited the cards during those years of employment, it is probably because someone asked what the vision for the company was, or because they were simply rummaging for a lost memory stick.

In other words, for the entire time that these people were employed, they haven't once connected with the aspiration of the company. If these were your own employees and you've been lucky, they have performed the tasks that they were employed to do efficiently, but they certainly haven't taken two steps at a time in the morning, and you probably haven't been getting the best out of them.

On the other hand, research indicates that if an organization has a compelling vision, one that truly connects employees with their work and motivates them toward a positive future, then that vision has a valuable, powerful, effect (Pinder 1998). The potential upside for the organization is enormous, impacting employees' work-related behaviors in "form, direction, intensity and duration. The level of commitment and motivation that an employee feels then becomes a resource-allocation process where time and energy are allocated to an array of tasks" (Pritchard and Payne 2003). So, the more connected employees are to the vision—the positive future state—the more likely they are to allocate their time and energy to the tasks of achieving the vision. For example, in the case of Kodak, it didn't require a giant leap in thinking for employees to understand what they could do as individuals to "make the camera as convenient as the pencil."

BELIEF LEADS TO COMMITMENT

Connecting to the vision of the organization creates organizational commitment, and one of the strongest and most predictable outcomes of employee commitment should be lower staff turnover rates (Mowday, Porter, and Steers 1982; Mathieu and Zajac 1990). In a more thorough review, the results of an extensive meta-analysis of the research supports this theory. Therefore, the most direct consequences of organizations creating compelling vision and engaging others around it is increased organizational commitment and lower staff turnover.

The indirect impact of a powerful vision that works for people is an increased productivity through the allocation of time and energy that each employee willingly attributes to the future of the organization. Where leaders are motivated primarily by numbers, they can still be convinced of the power of vision if they can see the correlation between higher levels of employee engagement and reduced staff turnover and absenteeism and increased productivity, and the impact these have on the bottom line.

A NEW MIND-SET AT WORK

A compelling vision will work for a large, well-known company like Microsoft, and it will also work for the small start-up email security company. The question remains, can it work for organizations that are in industries not typically considered exciting, such as banks, manufacturers, and government agencies? I met with Pete Delaney, a former Wall Street guy with several large public company CEO and board seats under his belt. Pete is a leader who does leading with vision well in an industry not typically considered exciting: energy production. During the meeting Pete shared his experience inside his organization and also how the same concepts could be translated into other areas, such as education.

At the time of our meeting, Pete was leading Enable Midstream through a transition. He had recently moved over from his CEO role at OGE Energy Corporation, a public utility where he was still chairman of the board. At OGE (Oklahoma Gas and Electric), Pete had served as CEO for seven years, and during that time the organization had experienced great success.

I asked Pete what he saw when an organization successfully connected a vision with its employees. In response, he described the implementation of the SmartHours program, a new initiative that OGE had launched to automatically adjust customers' thermostats during peak usage. This program was enabled by the development and integration of an innovative smart-grid technology platform, and it ultimately resulted in the company winning the Edison Award, the electric industry's most prestigious honor.

As Pete explained, in order to execute the SmartHours program, not only did the leaders need to motivate employees and customers to rally around a common goal, but they also needed to change the business strategy. In 2007, energy usage was on the rise, and future growth projections revealed the need to build a new power plant. New power generation also means increasing the environmental liability, and it's a huge investment that will inevitably hit every customer's monthly electric bill. However, those new power plants also increase earnings, and, traditionally, utilities hope to grow earnings through the construction of new power plants.

Pete said, "So there we were in 2007, almost at capacity and unwilling to risk investment in further capacity at that time. Throughout our history we had been telling employees to sell more energy but now we needed them to help us to reduce amount of energy our customers were using. When we first said it out loud, it sounded crazy."

Pete told me the objective was to change the direction of the company with a big, very bold, public goal: *big* to get attention, and *public* so that there was no backing down. However, Pete's next challenge was to engage the employees around the new direction.

They launched an all-out "skunkworks" project; that is, a project done in a set-aside business or department to keep it hidden from the public eye and allow it to act with speed by avoiding the standard bureaucracy. The result was a technology platform that allowed OGE to provide almost-real-time energy prices and use dynamic pricing to offer the customers the option of using the SmartHours thermostat adjustment program. For it to be successful, employees had to understand that the objective was to minimize price increases for customers in any way possible. All of the employees and all of the customers needed to engage. Generally, for regulated utilities in the past, price increases were associated with growing earnings. OGE was challenging the business model by finding ways to limit price increases. In addition, Pete said, "If we all came together on this, OGE could postpone the need to build the power plant for ten years."

In order to educate customers, OGE developed an education and communication campaign. "We had to change the mind-set," Pete said. "We used radio, television, social media, print, customer meetings, phone calls, and every method imaginable to educate the customers on how to manage their utility bill. In addition, there was a social and an environmental impact. As the message sunk in, the customers in particular felt empowered by the notion that their individual actions could delay an entire power plant for a decade. Everyone began to rally."

"So the 'no power plant until 2020' was the compelling vision that everyone rallied around?" I asked.

"Well, not exactly," Pete said. "It's interesting what connects people. While that was the ultimate destination, the compelling vision that captured everyone's heart was much closer to home. At OGE when we were starting this conversation, I went to Jean Leger, the vice president of Utility Operations, and said, 'We have to keep our costs flat despite growing investment and customer growth.' Jean tried several things before he and his team landed on the rally cry that united all of our employees: 'Protect the customer's bill.'"

I knew that what Pete was saying was true. Recently I had been on a leadership development project where I had met with more than fifty of the company's employees one-on-one for an hour or more. During many of those conversations, employees would make statements like, "We were working to protect the customer's bill," or, "I had to lead our department so that we were always protecting the customer's bill." One employee had even said, "After all, my mom is one of the customers."

The leadership of the business, the employees, and the customers were all connected to the organization through one unifying and personally compelling concept. The employees felt like they were making a difference, like they were an important character in the organization's story, and they were. Like the adage by Maya Angelou that Pete often shares: "I've learned that people will forget what you said, people will forget what you did, but people will never forget how you made them feel."

In this example, the employees were moved to solve a problem for their customers, for their families, and for their city. The protective nature of "Protect the customer's bill" resonated with the employees and with the regional culture. Pete didn't try to drive this kind of change with money. Instead, he and the other OGE leaders created an emotional spark that resonated with the employees, challenged them, made them feel a part of something bigger, and gave their work a purpose.

This unification ultimately resulted in OGE installing over 823,000 smart meters and enrolling more than 44,000 customers in the program. In addition, they were able to gain the needed load reduction by reducing usage by 72 megawatts during peak periods.

This effort was so successful that in August 2015, President Obama gave OGE kudos during his clean energy speech in Nevada: "Oklahoma Gas and Electric is empowering its customers to enroll in smart metering that uses electricity when it's cheaper, not when it's most expensive."

Expanding the Concept to Education

Hearing Pete's story, I felt inspired by the fact that such a profound outcome could result from vision and organizational connectedness in an industry that most would consider mundane. As I leaned back in my chair to listen to Pete, he said, "You know, Bonnie, there is another area where our employees rallied around a unifying concept: safety. In fact, I'm going to share the story tomorrow at the Oklahoma City Public Schools meeting of all principals, teachers, and staff."

"Go on," I said, reopening my notebook and reaching for a pen.

"Well, I want to make them think about what they do in a different light, one that hopefully will create a much more compelling vision and result in a commitment to make a greatly needed change in their culture. The school district has had a culture that seems to accept high dropout rates. The culture needs to be one that accepts nothing other than a graduation rate of 100 percent in the Oklahoma City School District."

Pete shared the message he planned to deliver the next day. "At OGE we protect our employees' lives, because we all believe that a 100 percent injury- and incident-free workplace is possible, especially in a hazardous environment where a simple mistake can take a life. Saving lives is very emotional, so I want to make my message tomorrow emotional for the teachers in a way that touches their heart. So my point will be that teachers will save lives if they believe a 100 percent graduation rate is possible. By getting these kids to graduation, they will ensure that the kids will be much more likely to avoid a life of poverty and drug use. I intend to share with the teachers the importance of building a strong culture based on a belief system that a 100 percent graduation rate is possible. Only with that belief will graduation rates substantially improve and children's lives be saved from the alternative."

Pete continued, "As you know, organizational culture is very important. It's our system of values and beliefs that drives our behaviors and actions. The men and women at OGE often work around energized equipment and in harsh conditions where mistakes in those circumstances can have deadly consequences. We take safety very seriously, and I'm sure you've experienced how devoted we are to our core value of living safely."

I certainly had, as no OGE employee will ever talk on the phone with me when I'm driving in my car, which happens to be my less-than-safe but undeniably best time to get a few calls in.

Pete continued to share that back in 2007 when he became CEO, they had approximately ninety safety incidents involving their employees. Incidents are injuries that require medical attention. Obviously, that was not acceptable. Safety has always been an OGE value. They talked a lot about safety and invested in equipment and procedures, but they were not really getting the results they wanted.

Pete described the process that he and his colleagues went through to understand how other sectors around the globe were dealing with the issue of safety. What they discovered was that while OGE had identified safety as a core value, they didn't have a *culture* of safety. "Our safety goal was to reduce the injuries from the year before," Pete said. "It was a continuous improvement approach. We had set a goal that basically said, 'Accidents are acceptable.'"

Pete explained that OGE leaders instinctively knew that accidents were not acceptable, and they recognized that their safety goal was not aligned with their intent, which was to eliminate all injuries and accidents. So, they adopted an incident-and-injury-free workplace goal, a goal of zero accidents and injuries. According to Pete, the zero goal surfaced in a lot of discussions, and those discussions revealed to us that we had a cultural mind-set that required some adjustment. Some leaders said, "that's not possible. That's why they are called accidents." But Pete and the leaders of OEG didn't give in. They didn't accept that the goal was impossible.

SAFETY FIRST

Pete spoke passionately about his role as a leader. "Accepting that accidents are not preventable lets us as leaders off the hook. If they are not preventable, then we are not responsible. But if we are not responsible, who is? We as leaders are responsible, because, in fact, all accidents are preventable. We have had people work for us forty years without an incident or injury. I believe that an injury-free workplace is possible."

He continued, "So we challenged our leaders and all of our employees to think about their safety belief and what they can do to protect others from injury. Only with an injury-free mentality and culture, with a goal of zero incidents, did we all understand our joint responsibility.

"As a part of the injury- and incident-free workplace journey, OGE had all employees write a letter to their families as if they were not ever going to make it home again due to a workplace injury, creating a very strong emotional response from each person as they realized the impact of their loss on others.

"Then we were able to make real progress. Because of that unifying safety commitment, our injury rate has improved dramatically. As of August 2015, we have had nine minor injuries. If we keep it up, before the year is over, we will have an 80 percent improvement from the 2007 number. It's not where we want to be, but it is a big leap forward. We identified the underlying problem and tackled it head on, keeping the issue alive until it was fully embedded into the culture and clear progress could be measured.

"This is what I'm going to share with the Oklahoma City School District tomorrow," Pete said. "I believe that they can have a graduation rate of 100 percent. Hopefully they can believe it as well. I'm not sure if that helps you identify what it takes to make a compelling vision, but those are two examples where I've seen employees become completely engaged and personally connected around a vision—not necessarily the company's stated vision but maybe something even more important."

Keeping people safe was an issue that rallied people. Once again, it wasn't an issue of money. As John, Simon, and I examined the components of these examples at the sharp end where the work is actually happening—and not in the classroom in a case study—we debated whether or not the examples that Pete described were visions, missions, or goals. There are many definitions for vision, mission, and goals, but they all mean basically the same thing. In our own words, we describe them like this:

- Vision: A clear picture of a positive future state
- Mission: Why are we here? Why do we exist?
- Goals: The bite-size pieces that get the organization to the positive future state

Both of Pete's examples could be considered a positive future state, so we agreed that they were compelling visions. They did not serve as the overarching vision statement for the company, but they were compelling nonetheless. However, the discussion didn't end there. The very next question we asked was, "Does it matter? Does it really matter whether it is technically a vision, mission, or goal?"

I'll spare you the passionate debate that ensued, but let's just say we were noisy, and eventually we all decided we were passionately debating the same side of the argument. We don't think it matters whether you use the term *vision*, *mission*, *purpose*, *goal*, or anything else, as long as it works for you and your industry. What matters most is that your employees are inspired; they feel personally connected to the story; they feel like key characters in the story; they get excited; and they come to work taking the stairs two steps at a time.

TAKEAWAYS FROM CHAPTER 2

- Think about the organization you want to create and how you want people to feel about working there. What is your equivalent of "taking the stairs two at a time"?

- Create a compelling vision and visualize the future state so that you can describe it for employees. Remember to paint a picture with your words. Make it very clear.

- As a leader, own the vision and be responsible for ensuring that everyone understands it.

- Know that connected, engaged people are more productive and less likely to leave—it makes good financial sense.

CHAPTER 3

Who Gets Connectedness Right?

O UR WORK AROUND VISION became ever richer and more stimulating as we gained insights and pushed past our own preconceived notions, asking more questions of ourselves, of the research, and of the leaders who were doing the work. The more we looked, the more we understood that personally feeling connected to the story of the organization is core, so we looked for leaders and organizations who had been successful in this area.

We identified St. Luke's University and Health Network in Pennsylvania as an organization that gets it right when it comes to making sure that employees feel like a part of the story. I arranged to meet with Rick Anderson, the long-standing CEO of St. Luke's, and traveled to meet him in Bethlehem, Pennsylvania, a beautiful place known as the Christmas City. Bethlehem is the former home of the Bethlehem Steel Corporation, home of the Moravian Church, and the oldest bookstore in the country. Rick Anderson can be counted among the few healthcare CEOs with such a long success record. He has held the position for more than thirty years, whereas the average healthcare CEO tenure is five and a half years.

I hadn't been to St. Luke's for several years, but I knew it well from working closely with their leaders between 2001 and 2007. Rick met me at the Richard A. Anderson Campus, which was named after him, where he gave me a tour of the $200 million campus, including the 100-plus-bed hospital. It was the newest addition to the St. Luke's network—the sixth in Anderson's thirty-year leadership career—and the seventh was already in progress.

The campus was beautiful and welcoming, built on 200 acres with another 300 acres of lush farmland across the highway. Every detail of the patients' care is covered here. The hospital employs top-rated physicians and nurses and maintains the highest-quality equipment and facilities. The surrounding environment includes natural restorative properties where patients, employees, and volunteers can take a walk, sit by the lake, or get their hands in the dirt tending the community herb garden.

As we began the tour, I insisted that Rick let me take his picture beside the commissioned portrait of him in the foyer. I couldn't help thinking that this sort of recognition is usually afforded only to those who have made multimillion-dollar donations or are being fondly remembered after passing away.

BRAND INITIATIVE

I knew from my work there that employees were profoundly connected to St. Luke's as an organization. The culture at St. Luke's makes employees feel core to the St. Luke's story and like an important part of the mission. In 2006, St. Luke's conducted a brand identity initiative which culminated in the *My Health, My St. Luke's* promotional campaign. I wanted to hear from Rick and his team about the employee connectedness, and after talking for a while, we both felt that the 2006 branding effort was important, because it managed to capture the essence of who they are.

When they first started this initiative, Bob Martin, the chief strategy officer, hired Susan Dubuque from Neathawk, Dubuque & Packett, an advertising, marketing, and public relations agency, to come and help them put words to the St. Luke's story. Susan and her team put the organization through a rigorous brand development process, which started internally with the leadership team. They conducted a wide range of interviews and then moved on to focus groups with physicians, board members, volunteers, and employees, careful to keep managers and line staff separate so they would get the full and honest story.

I called Susan to learn more about this approach. She explained how they wanted to understand the mission, the strategic plan, and the vision "because we want the brand to be aspirational." She noted that in the end it had to be very credible with all of the key stakeholders, especially the employees deep in the organization. If it resonated with them, there would be alignment.

Once Susan's team felt they understood the internal perceptions and state of the organization, they went external, conducting both qualitative and quantitative research to understand how St. Luke's was perceived in the community. This meant not only understanding St. Luke's as a healthcare provider and as one of Lehigh Valley's largest employers, but also determining why people choose St. Luke's over others, such as Lehigh Valley Health Network, a formidable competitor as well as an aggressive marketer. Their approach contrasted with St. Luke's, who tended to expect their care and service to be their best marketing asset.

Susan's team also reviewed other secondary data, such as market share and referral source. When the data analysis was complete, they called the St. Luke's leadership team together for a brand summit to zero in on what made St. Luke's special. The brand identity had to meet several criteria:

- Is it credible?
- Is it compelling?
- Is it distinguishing?
- Does it apply to all of our products and services?
- Does it present a benefit to the consumer?

CULTURE: THE BRAND'S FOUNDATION

In order to understand how Susan's team ultimately ended up creating a brand that resonated so well, we wanted to understand how they were able to put words to the culture. It seemed a difficult task because they had uncovered such a deep well of information. Consequently, the fact that they were able to put words to it surprised and impressed me. Susan

Dubuque shared how they really tried to just listen without any precon-ceived ideas. They focused on St. Luke's and who they really are.

What they found is a St. Luke's where the culture is personal, collabor-ative, and caring, and that these characteristics really resonated with their community and employees. *My Health, My St. Luke's* captured the respect that the organization shows to everyone, from consumers to employees and ultimately to the greater community. The brand let consumers assume responsibility for their own health and wellness in partnership with St. Luke's. Today this is much more commonplace in healthcare, but at the time it was a true paradigm shift. The brand is very respectful, because the employees and volunteers of St. Luke's are very respectful people. They are your partner in healthcare, and anyone who has been to any of the St. Luke's network hospitals knows that. As they say at St. Luke's, "When you walk in, you can feel it. It's genuine and palpable." The *My Health, My St. Luke's* brand identity and subsequent marketing campaign was right on target. There was clearly something about this organization that made it a compelling place to work, with many of their employees stay-ing for their entire careers and some even coming on board as second- or third-generation employees. *My Health, My St. Luke's* captured something important about the unity and connectedness of the organization.

PAYING ATTENTION

As Rick gave me the tour of the new and beautiful campus, we walked through the hallways, stopping to check out the high-tech hospital rooms. He paused to talk to every single employee along the way. If he didn't know them by name (there are over 9,500 employees, operating from over 200 service sites under his leadership), he introduced himself, and me, and told them why we were there. He also asked how they were doing. When we came to a patient check-in area, Rick noticed a small sign notifying patients to pay their co-pay up front. He picked it up, read it, and frowned.

"I don't like the tone," he said. "It is too demanding. Surely there's another way to say that." Then he made a call. I didn't go there the next day, but I'm guessing that sign was gone.

The next morning, I met with Rick again for a formal interview. Pondering the connectedness employees had to St. Luke's, I walked the halls to go to Rick's office. I noticed the pictures of nurses, doctors, patients, and buildings dating back to the early 1900s. They hung on both sides of the hall and went back over the 100-plus-year history of the foundational hospital. Most of the employees passed those pictures every day as they made their way to and from the parking garage, and the photos served as a continuous reminder that they were a part of something long-standing and important in the community. The facilities may have been cutting edge but this wasn't a start-up; it had a history and a responsibility.

During the interview, Rick complimented his long-term executive assistant, Donna Fields. "I don't know what I would do without her." She came in several times during the interview, knowing exactly where to find a newspaper article or a detail he didn't have. "She's one of the reasons we have been so successful."

Later Rick told me about his wife, Helen. He said she was one of the reasons he had been able to successfully lead St. Luke's for thirty years. Before the interview was over, he had also said the same about his board and his senior leadership team and the employees. The only person he left out was himself.

While I was there to talk about the *My Health, My St. Luke's* initiative and what connected employees to St. Luke's, it was clear that Rick was a huge driver of the culture. I realized later, when I reviewed the interview with my coauthors, that we would need to determine if the connector was Rick, the mission, the vision for growth, or all of it.

LEADERSHIP THAT EMPOWERS

Rick stepped out of his office to answer a question as another one of his leaders, Dean Evans, president of St. Luke's Physician Group,[1] stepped in to say hello. I had worked with Dean for years, and it was good to see him

---

[1] For further information see St. Luke's website, *About St. Luke's University Health Network, www.slhn.org/About.*

again. With Rick out of the room, I took the opportunity to ask Dean what compelled him to work at St. Luke's. He didn't hesitate.

"Him," he said, motioning toward Rick in the other room.

"Why him?" I asked.

"Because he empowers me to do what I need to do to get the right physicians for our network and build the organization to handle their practices. He lets me do my thing."

From this exchange, it may seem that Rick is a passive leader, but that isn't the case at all. He is a very assertive person who is straightforward and competitive. He has a vision and a way he wants things to go, but he doesn't rule with an iron fist. He has built a strong and cohesive leadership team, and as Dean said, he lets them "do their thing."

Previously, Rick had shared a story with me about a leader who had left to join another organization for a bigger title and more money. Rick said at the time, "There are great leaders here, but when you're here (and I include myself in this statement) you can be very successful because of the St. Luke's team. Sometimes people think they'll be just as successful in another organization, but they leave and then they find out the real importance of the St. Luke's dynamic." The team is stronger than the leader and the leader's job is to create a great team. That is the philosophy Rick has lived by all these years, and it has served him well.

"Learning means making mistakes, and if we stop learning we're in trouble."

—Rick A. Anderson, CEO, St. Luke's

We went on to discuss a CFO who had recently left. I asked if the leader had left for seemingly greener pastures.

"No," Rick said, shaking his head, "that was my fault. I hired the CFO because I felt like we needed a heavy hitter to handle the aggressive growth and strategy work. The person I hired had been a trusted adviser to the organization for many years. However, when I brought this person into the organization as a leader, it wasn't a good fit.

"The job had been open for a period of time with an internal leader, Tom Lichtenwalner, acting as the interim CFO. Tom also had expressed interest in the job. However, at the time I felt a leader needed to come from the outside.

"When I realized my mistake, I went to Tom. I told him I accepted full responsibility and that I would fix the problem. Tom is now the CFO and performing in an outstanding manner. I hope that my team knows that I'm willing to admit my mistakes, just as I expect them to admit their own. If they aren't making mistakes, then they aren't doing enough to learn and grow. Learning means making mistakes, and if we stop learning we're in trouble."

A VISIONARY LEADER

As is the case in many organizations, the connector for the employees at St. Luke's was heavily weighted toward a strong visionary leader, and the *My Health, My St. Luke's* brand emerged as the voice of the DNA Rick had formed and all had embraced. To emphasize the point, Rick's assistant, Donna, handed me this email from an employee.

I have been reading all the publications and interviews celebrating your 30 years of service. I just want to tell you that I concur with your assessment of our organization. I spent only 6½ years as an employee and am now a contractor helping out. Over my 30+ year career as a nurse and within finance, I spent time at six different organizations in three states, I can honestly say that St. Luke's far exceeds every other experience for me in terms of working in a positive, rewarding culture that lives its mission. I have always had a passion for healthcare and the delivery of it to the underserved population, and at St. Luke's I was able to expand programs benefitting that population with full support from senior leadership. I was able to implement incentive programs for staff and help create the Pre-Encounter Center and the Call Ahead Lab Program because of leaders who listened, were not afraid to take a chance, and supported these efforts. I never felt a fear of failing and the consequences that might negatively impact me or my reputation.

You set the tone for this and it filters through the organization. You allow individualism to flourish and not only accept differences in style but actually encourage the synergy that this creates. I loved every moment of my time as an employee and am enjoying my new role and the opportunity to continue to help the organization in any way I can during these challenging times. I wanted to tell you this and thank you for your service to our organization and our wonderful community.

This was quite an endorsement. This former employee never mentioned a salary or a retirement plan. It was all about loving the work at St. Luke's because it was rewarding. The employee's passion was fulfilled by the ability to develop meaningful programs and by the leaders who cared enough to listen. There was so much support, this employee lost the fear of failure.

St. Luke's is definitely a place where employees feel connected. It is compelling, but is it actually a compelling *vision*? The components for employee connectedness in this case were a caring and compelling leader, a deep understanding of being a part of something greater than themselves, a sense of being a part of the community for over 100 years, and the altruistic concept of being a part of the patient's very personal healthcare. All of this aligned perfectly with the brand of St. Luke's, which was so aptly captured in the *My Health, My St. Luke's* campaign.

On the one hand, St. Luke's was focused on growth, and it had actually grown significantly from a single hospital to a healthcare network, including the establishment of a regional medical school campus with Temple University School of Medicine. However, that didn't seem to be the connector for employees. On the other hand, the growth was intended to deliver better-quality healthcare to more people, which was a connector and motivator. The vision for St. Luke's that has been written down and filed away isn't nearly as inspiring as the vision Rick talks about and with which his colleagues engage. What is more, we realized that St. Luke's was actually beyond the point of needing a compelling vision because they have already succeeded in creating a compelling culture that continually strives toward the vision and the mission and one that is achieving what so many other organizations are striving for.

THE SOCCER-PLAYING CEO AND
THE TURNAROUND

Simon had another leader for us to study, a soccer-playing CEO from San Diego. His name was Chris Lischewski, the CEO of Bumble Bee Seafoods,[2] an organization founded in 1899 and a primary supplier of albacore tuna, salmon, sardines, and other specialty seafood products. Simon had interviewed Chris in 2015, and as John, Simon, and I reviewed his notes, we were able to see a completely different picture than what we had seen with St. Luke's. This time, the leader had a vision, set the course, and then put together a team that would be compelled to run the course.

Simon had worked with Bumble Bee two years earlier on a couple of assignments that had included multiple interviews with people in the organization. This gave him a very good feel for the culture. When he worked with Chris at the company, they walked the halls together. Simon thought Chris was very engaging. Chris stopped along the way and visited with the employees as they went. But Simon also noticed that Chris was a tough leader who insisted on strong performance.

Simon and Chris also play soccer together, and Simon was aware that Chris is very competitive and always wants to win. At the same time, Chris is very charismatic and quite generous. After one soccer match in Las Vegas, the teams went out for drinks. They sat at separate tables, and the losing team bought Chris' team a round of drinks. Not to be outdone, Chris reciprocated within minutes. His competitive nature just couldn't let them get one up on him, not even for a free drink. This was on top of the fact that he also paid for the entire tournament, including all of the

---

[2] For further information see the Bumblebee website, *All About Bumble Bee*, *www.bumblebee.com/about-us/*.

team jerseys. As Simon linked Chris's on- and off-the-field mannerisms, it was clear that his competitive nature was also an important part of the Bumble Bee story.

Chris took the helm at Bumble Bee in September 1999. He inherited an organization that was coming out of several years of bankruptcy. The culture was poor. Most of the people were substandard performers, lacked motivation, or both. In fact, many of the people who were still there were those who couldn't get a job elsewhere. The company had one core product line on which they were over-reliant, and the industry itself was very fragmented.

Chris shared that he had to rebuild and expand the product lines, rebuild the culture, and rebuild the team. Over a painful eighteen-month process, he learned how difficult and how important it is to put the right team together. He told Simon, "Initially, I guess I thought I could do the turnaround myself, but it didn't take long to realize I had to put together a management team that worked. It's all about the people. You can give me a bad company with good people, and we will figure out how to make money. Not one person in the management team today was there when I started."

Ultimately they had to completely rebuild, and hiring right is rarely easy. Chris believes that when you get into the mode where you're hiring workers, you have to understand that hiring isn't just about skills and competencies, you have to hire people who will fit into the culture. And that's even harder to do if, as the leader, you haven't created the culture yet. In general, you'll know within three months if someone is a good fit or not. At that point, Chris said, "If it's not the right person, cut bait and move on." It was a tough lesson for Chris.

COMPETITIVE CHALLENGE

As a serious sports competitor, Chris was used to challenges. He even thrived on them, but a turnaround of this magnitude was a lot for even the bravest of leaders. He knew he was going to need a special group of people to take a mismanaged brand and lead this organization out of bankruptcy and into his vision of being the leader among seafood companies. Competitive sports players understand the need for and power of both vision and a cohesive team, so Chris set out to create both. He hired people who had a winning mentality, including many current and former athletes. This was not a job for the faint of heart, so he knew that his team members would need to have strong spirits.

Chris expounded on the vision. He knew that in order to be the leading brand in the industry, they had to do more than just reestablish the brand on the shelves in the supermarket. The brand had to mean something to consumers and to employees. He said, "I saw that the population was becoming more and more focused on health and wellness. We wanted to be a part of that move, a contributor. We decided to lead in sustainability and conservation and to push the industry so that consumers expected that from everyone in our category."

Chris ensured that every manager and every employee understood the mission in these areas. Because of their financial predicament, the real challenge began when they had to drive sustainability and conservation without adding cost to the business. But they still had to do it. It had to be a continuous part of the business. They wanted to be proud of their products, and they wanted their customers to feel good about purchasing them. And, of course, Chris needed a strong and competent team who could do it.

TEAM BUILDING

Chris reflected on the process of building the winning team. He said, "Putting the right team together was my biggest challenge. I had to have powerful leaders who could hire and develop other powerful leaders and employees. The precedents I set early on were strong communication and complete transparency. We set constant, systematic, and thorough lines of communication. Just like on the soccer field, a business team has to be in constant communication and fully aware of what is going on in other parts of the game. People who have played competitive sports understand this. That is one of the reasons I tend to hire people who have that in their background, because they learn to play on a team. They learn to win, and they learn to not like losing."

Chris also reasoned that there had to be a lot of trust among his organization's teams. In order to achieve this, they chose to be fully transparent with all employees. There was no smoke and mirrors. Every employee had to understand the predicament the business was in and what Chris was doing to address it.

Chris explained, "We are a private company, so we don't disclose our financials externally, but we do disclose our financials to all of our employees. They all have the right to know, both the good and the bad."

Chris felt the employees needed to see how the organization was doing, just like the leaders. He believed that they were all in it together. "It's our team and our company and everyone needs to know the score."

On the other hand, it is a two-way street. The employees also have to be fully engaged and playing in their own position on the team at 100 percent. If the opponent is weak, team members can get away with 80 percent effort, but Bumble Bee was in a game against big odds, and the entire team needed to play at 100 percent.

With this in mind, Chris and his team set the vision to be the leading brand in their industry. They had a social responsibility mission. They built a strong team, and they went after their goal with their whole heart.

BUMBLE BEE BRAND

And the result? They did a complete and successful turnaround. Today Bumble Bee Foods is the largest branded, shelf-stable seafood company in North America. They eliminated additives, eliminated preservatives, and eliminated salt in their foods. They also implemented a strong medical benefits program for the employees that is designed for proactive health awareness and active versus reactive healthcare. And in the social responsibility part of their business, they are continuously leading initiatives to ensure sustainable management of tuna fisheries as well as the greater challenge of improving overall ocean health.

Chris's competitive sports background likely played a role in Bumble Bee's success both because of his competitive nature and because, as we stated earlier, athletes are trained to do visualization. Chris visualized what he wanted the company to be and helped his team visualize it as well.

VISUALIZING SUCCESS

In sports, the visualization process is extremely ingrained into the practice routines of the athlete. For example, Kristi Overton Johnson is a retired professional athlete. She was the world record holder in women's slalom from 1992 through 2010, and she was recently inducted into the USA Water Ski Hall of Fame and the North Carolina Sports Hall of Fame. I know from talking to Kristi that visualizing her water ski routine was one of the most important parts of her training. Her visualization work started when she was very young. Her father, Parker Overton, sat beside her each night and told her bedtime stories, which he made up. The stories had "little Kristi" as the famous water skier, and they always had her winning against her competitors. Not only was her father teaching her to visualize, but also she was the main character in the story and therefore engaged and desirous of a positive outcome.

Kristi's visualization work continued during each practice session, where her father, as well as her coaches, taught her to train each day as if she was in a tournament and ski each tournament as if she was in practice. They wanted her to envision herself at the tournament as she practiced so that the routine would be well positioned in her mind when she actually skied the tournament. They also had her train with men versus women and compete at their level, so her visualization and her actual practice included a competition much harder than she might face. Then when the time came, just before each tournament, she would go see the ski lake where the tournament was held, so she could picture herself on it. She visualized every move, every buoy, over and over again. She visualized herself skiing a perfect run and then coming up in a fist pump and, in the end, winning and standing on the podium.

Kristi visualized her routine so much that her mother saw her going through her routine in her sleep when they stayed together in the hotels before each tournament. Such was the power of visualization that when Kristi was injured at one of the Masters tournaments and couldn't practice, she just lay flat on her back in the hotel and visualized the ski run over and over again. Though injured, she was able to ski the actual competition run, and she skied it perfectly, even though she hadn't practiced in days. She said that creating and living the vision for skiing was so embedded into her that even today, years after she professionally retired, she can still feel every twist and turn in her ski routine.

From an Individual Vision to a Collective Vision

In a company, a vision that can't be visualized is just a statement. The ability to collectively visualize the positive future state helps employees to prepare for and achieve the vision. It helps to put word pictures around where the company is going. Just think about a wall with a painting hanging on it. Imagine that the painting is slightly crooked, maybe thirty degrees off. What do you want to do? If you are like most people, you want to straighten the picture. Why? Because you have a mental idea in your mind about how a painting should hang on a wall. If all of your employees have a mental idea about what success looks like concerning the vision for your organization, then any time something is a little off from what is needed to get there, your employees will want to straighten it. They will want to help the organization get to the successful place, one they have collectively visualized. This approach creates an unstoppable force. As Kristi had shown, once you start visualizing you don't stop; the picture stays with you sometimes even long after you need it.

THE BRAND AND THE VISION

With Bumble Bee, Chris was able to implement what he had learned in sports: both the desire to win and the ability to visualize winning. He painted the mental picture for the employees: to be the leading brand. Then he went about putting the pieces into place to achieve the vision.

As Simon worked with Bumble Bee, he found the leaders were very engaged and compelled to reach the vision of being the leading brand, which in their case meant the largest. They were also very connected to the sustainability and conservation messages.

Chris created a vision—though not in and of itself compelling—and he hired people who would be compelled to overcome the enormous odds they had against them and reach the goal. What connected the employees was a really big challenge. Chris put together a team of people who know how to tackle and enjoy a big challenge, a team of people who don't like to lose. They were like warriors who wanted to get in the fight. It was the battle that was compelling as well as the social responsibility.

Bumble Bee isn't a lifelong-mission-type environment like St. Luke's, where employees often dedicate their entire careers to the organization, so we wondered what reaching the goal would mean for Chris' team. John, Simon, and I assumed that once the goal was met, he would either need to find a different team that could connect to the process of structure and keep it running smoothly, or he would need a new challenge. But Chris is not a "keep things running smoothly" kind of guy. He likes a challenge and feels there is still plenty to do with Bumble Bee, whether it's new products, new markets, or just growing market share. For Chris, there should always be a goal to reach, and if there isn't, he'll probably move on and look for a new challenge. In that way, Chris is very similar to Gen Y.

As my coauthors and I reviewed the stories of St. Luke's and Bumble Bee in preparation for writing this chapter, we immediately recognized that the leaders of St. Luke's and Bumble Bee achieved success in very different ways. Rick created a culture, which employees bought into, and Chris set an audacious challenge that galvanized his team. Looking beyond these two stories, however, we wondered if either approach would be enough to engage with the emerging workforce. We knew that connectedness was one component of the ability to lead with vision—but what were the others? What was really needed to succeed if leaders were to ride the tidal wave of change sweeping across today's organizations?

Fortunately, we had a vital tool to turn to as we continued to explore these questions: we knew that the *Trends* research, along with other related research, would help us gain the additional insight we needed. We report the results of our findings in chapter 4.

TAKEAWAYS FROM CHAPTER 3

- Surround yourself with great people and make it your job to help them develop.
- Know the characteristics and attributes of the people you want in your organization, because not everyone will be right for you.
- Notice the details and don't allow anything to undermine the culture you want to create.
- Connect with people—personally—every day.
- Visualize what success looks like, and find ways to articulate what you are visualizing.

CHAPTER 4

Visionary Leadership at Work

A S JOHN, SIMON, AND I began to zero in on what attributes leaders need to possess in order to be able to create a compelling vision and engage others around it, we took a deep dive into the *Trends*—the results of the 2016 EDA *Trends in Executive Development* research. With every biennial analysis, the research reveals clear leadership needs that either are, or are not, being dealt with effectively in year-over-year comparisons. The reports that come out of the research are benchmark reports so that organizations can use them to compare their own work and needs with those of others. When we see that a need isn't improving over time, we know we have to get better at helping leaders bridge the gap. This is certainly the case with creating a compelling vision and engaging others around it. The chart below from the 2016 *Trends* research shows that the ability to create a compelling vision and engage others around it has been one of the top three most lacking competencies in next-generation leaders since 2009 (see Figure 1).

And yet, when it comes down to what gets top priority in executive development, this competency only just made the top five list (at number 5) in 2015 (see Figure 2). According to this, there is a conflict between what is urgent versus what is important. It is urgent that organizations focus on real business issues and challenges facing them today, which means that the activities that are important and necessary for long-term success—such as developing leaders who can create a compelling vision and engage others around it—get pushed down the list of priorities. This is not

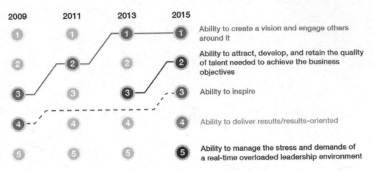

Figure 1. The top 5 competencies most lacking in the next generation of leaders.

Source: Hagemann, 18

unusual, of course, because each one of us struggles with the same priority challenge every day. The latest email gets answered while the much-needed difficult conversation gets pushed to the back burner. Organizations as a whole experience the same challenge around their priorities.

There is a need to address the balance, and hopefully in the coming years we will begin to bridge the gap and help our next-generation leaders take the helm effectively.

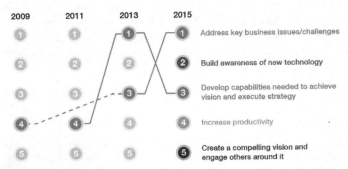

Figure 2. The top priorities of executive development in the next 2 to 3 years.

Source: Hagemann, 20

Upon taking a closer look at the data, we asked ourselves a few questions. If the task of creating a vision and engaging others around it is one of the skills most lacking in the next generation of leaders, then

1. Why is it not more of a priority when it comes to the development of leaders?
2. What is it in practice that leaders actually need to get better at doing?

The more we studied the related research and interviewed successful visionary leaders who could rally the troops, the more the pieces of the puzzle began to fall into place.

Top Five Most-Needed Competencies in Next-Generation Leaders

1. Ability to create a vision and engage others around it
2. Ability to attract, develop, and retain the quality of talent needed to achieve the business objectives
3. Ability to inspire
4. Ability to deliver results/results oriented
5. Ability to manage the stress and demand of the real-time overloaded leadership environment

---

Much has been written about leadership, vision, engagement, the constant turbulence of change, and even the emergence of a new workforce. However, our understanding of what it means in the twenty-first century to provide engaging, visionary leadership to everyone in the organization—and to use this to unleash people's energy and potential—is much less understood ("Millennials at Work: Reshaping the Workplace" 2011). Our *Trends* research highlighted this fact.

We knew the steps needed to create a compelling vision, but we also wanted to understand the primary leadership techniques that every leader in every organization can use to engage the employees around the vision. It's one thing to have a great vision, but it is entirely something else to get others to buy in and be compelled to help achieve the vision. While recognizing that effective leadership is too multidimensional to believe that this captures everything needed, we did identify the essential elements without which engaging the workforce will be extremely difficult if not impossible. They are courage, clarity, connectedness, and culture. These are not leadership qualities but rather approaches to leadership. There are leadership qualities that are needed as well, and these are covered in other works, notably Kouzes and Posner's (2012) bestselling book *The Leadership Challenge: How to Make Extraordinary Things Happen in Organizations*. In the fifth edition Kouzes and Posner discuss their comprehensive research on the topic, and one of the questions they asked respondents was "What do you look for and admire in a leader, someone whose direction you would willingly follow?" Four qualities, and only four, have been selected by over 60 percent of respondents during the entire 30 years of Kouzes' and Posner's research. These qualities are: Honest, Forward-looking, Competent, and Inspiring (Kouzes and Posner 2012). Important lessons derived from their research were: [1] Credibility is the foundation of leadership (this relates to the qualities of honest and competent, in particular); and [2] Being forward-looking is the quality that differentiates leaders from individual contributors. Constituents want their leaders to know where they are going and be able to articulate a vision for the future in such a way they can see themselves in the picture. In addition to their research on what people want from their leaders, Kouzes and Posner have also researched and written extensively about what leaders do when they are performing at their best. One of their Five Practices of Exemplary Leadership® is "inspire a shared vision." Their work points to the fact that leaders must "envision the future by imagining exciting and ennobling possibilities" and "enlist others in a common vision by appealing to shared aspirations." Their findings lend support to our research on what leaders must do to effectively engage the workforce around a vision, and that is to:

1. Embody courage.
2. Forge clarity.
3. Build connectedness.
4. Shape culture.

Let's examine each approach one by one.

EMBODY COURAGE

Setting a compelling vision takes courage in three important ways. First, leaders must have the courage to be bold: to chart a new course, take risks, and potentially fail. Second, leaders must have the courage to be vulnerable. Third is the courage to stand firm, which is intrinsic to being bold and vulnerable but is a quality that might be called upon more often on a day-to-day basis.

Being Bold

It may seem to the outsider that organizational leaders are naturally bold. After all, isn't that how they made it to the leadership role in the first place? But that isn't always the case. In fact, it can be difficult to find bold leaders who make courageous decisions in the face of adversity and risk.

We saw in the last chapter how Chris Lischewski from Bumble Bee Seafoods established a bold vision—from almost nothing to market leader. What is it about leaders who are bold and make courageous decisions that engage a workforce better than those who don't?

Courage, by definition, is the mental or moral strength to venture, persevere, and withstand danger, fear, or difficulty ("Courage" n.d.). Leaders will tell you that vision is hard, and that one of the reasons for this is because it requires the courage to set bigger goals and go into uncharted territory, but also to understand risk and moderate it effectively as each new path is mapped. It means leaders have to take their eye off of shareholder returns and other top priorities long enough to figure out which mountain they need to climb next.

> *"Courage is the main quality of leadership, in my*
> *opinion, no matter where it is exercised. Usually it*
> *implies some risk—especially in new undertakings."*
>
> —Walt Disney

People like courageous leaders. We find them fascinating, and the success of enduring organizations and institutions is largely attributed to their leaders. As human beings, we seem to have an innate need for leadership. When we can't find it, we drift and become disenchanted, and we wait. When a courageous person steps into the leadership gap, we rally. We get excited. We want to follow. We just want the leader to be worth following. Courageous leaders give us hope.

Unfortunately, courage is not tangible. It is subjective—but we know it when we see it. It seems to live somewhere between bold and reckless. In *Nicomachean Ethics*, Aristotle (2009) describes courage as the fine line between fear and audacity; an excess of fear leads to cowardice and an excess of audacity to recklessness. We respect leaders who make a bold decision that puts their own job at risk; we do not respect leaders who make reckless decisions that put everyone's job at risk.

Being Vulnerable

This is the second type of courage. Potentially as difficult as the courage to be bold and probably even more frightening, being vulnerable in this context means being exposed and sharing your passion, excitement, and concerns for the organization, the vision, and the employees. It means being honest, authentic, and open. As seen in the Kouzes and Posner (2012) research cited earlier, we want our leaders to be honest. It's inspiring when we know that a leader feels pain and yet leads through the pain.

For example, we admire leaders like Sir Richard Branson, who gave a thoughtful but determined response when faced with catastrophe in October 2014, when his company, Virgin Galactic, suffered a tragedy. One of their pilots, Mike Alsbury, was killed during a test flight of Galactic's commercial spacecraft. Sir Richard explained that he seriously questioned whether or not it was worth continuing, but that it was "the designers, the builders, the engineers, the pilots and the whole community who passionately believed—and still believe—that truly opening space and making it accessible and safe is of vital importance to all our futures" (Howell 2015).

Difficult decisions come with courageous leadership, but here we see a leader who did it well. Richard Branson shared his own pain, his own questioning. He listened carefully and thoughtfully to the key stakeholders. Then he stepped forward and made a brave decision to continue in the face of adversity. He modeled courageous leadership.

Further vulnerability lies in empowerment. In the *Trends* research, one of the key developments identified by 466 leading organizations around the world is that businesses and leaders operate in the VUCA world (Volatile, Uncertain, Complex, Ambiguous) described previously in chapter 1 (Hagemann et al. 2016). In this environment, a new kind of leadership is required: whereas empowerment was valuable in the past, now it is crucial. The work environment is simply changing too fast. Customers are much more knowledgeable than ever before, and often organizations are too big for top-down leadership in an age where speed of response is what customers want and expect.

The courageous leader's job is about empowerment. The role is shifting to one of setting the stage, providing support and challenge, and ensuring alignment, rather than making every decision.

Leaders have to create agility within their organizations, which means empowerment. But empowerment is one area of potential vulnerability; in fact, it is frightening for many leaders. They want to ensure that the right decisions are made, to have a say in the decisions, and, often, to make those final decisions themselves. The simple truth, however, is that in today's speed-addicted environment, by the time the issue makes it to a senior leader, it's old news. The customer has already moved on, or the need is no longer the same. Courageous leaders are setting the guiding vision, creating the right environment, establishing and explaining the values with which everyone works, communicating overall intent, sharing as much information as possible, and then empowering those who are closest to the work to make on-the-spot decisions. An organization where most decisions have to be made at the top is now a sign of a weak leader, because a strong leader ensures that the organization is so clear about the vision, values, and purpose that the employees closest to the work can be trained for and trusted to make the right decision.

Standing Firm

Finally, leaders require the courage to stand firm and demonstrate strength without appearing stubborn or reckless. Standing firm is part of being bold and vulnerable, but your boldness and vulnerability might only be interpreted by others as being resolute and steady, which is a good thing. There is a common notion that it is courageous to maintain consistent behavior under increasing levels of adversity. Just think of a situation where a leader emerged in dire circumstances. Was that leader seemingly calm, clear, and consistent? That type of leadership feels courageous and steady. It feels trustworthy. This comes back to the need for honesty and, ultimately, behavioral integrity; leaders who follow through in spite of new challenges are seen as more courageous (Simons et al. 2007).

FORGE CLARITY

Forging clarity requires the leader to show empathy, which involves understanding the other person's position and communicating in terms that the other person easily understands. The visionary leader must present the vision with complete clarity if the organization's leaders and employees are to understand where they need to take the organization and what they need to do. Of course, it seems obvious that a leader needs to be clear about the message. However, although it is fundamental, it isn't as simple as it seems.

Clarity of an organization's vision requires layers of thought and attention. For example, first there must be vision clarity. That is the very clear and compelling positive future state, such as in Virgin Galactic's plan to open space and make it accessible and safe. Then there is communication clarity, which involves sharing the vision in a way that others hear it as it is meant to be heard. This is especially important. Have you ever tried to read Shakespeare out loud? I have and despite having the words in front of me I can never get the rhythm right, so the phrasing sounds clunky and I emphasize the wrong words. But give the text to a classical actor and suddenly the words have meaning; what sounded like gibberish from my mouth is crystal clear when it is delivered the right way. With communication clarity, what we are listening for is a message that is so clear it effortlessly travels through the organization and is immediately understood by everyone.

The reasons visions are often not communicated clearly are many, but we often see them fall on deaf ears because the vision is not truly in the heart of the leaders, or the leaders have not taken the time needed to ensure that the message is extremely clear. This is where visualization can really help leaders to achieve clarity.

If vision clarity and communication clarity are achieved, then practical goals and action can follow. However, the need for clarity continues. In particular, there needs to be *role* clarity so that everyone knows their place, *process* clarity in that employees need to know what processes will and will not be used to achieve the vision, and *decision-making* clarity in order to know when and by whom decisions will be made.

Our examination of related research shows that clarity and commitment to goals help teams align their creative processes with their objectives, with the result that all members are pulling in the same direction (Weingart and Weldon 1991). Getting employees to be clear about their role in achieving the vision and to be committed to pulling in the same direction is crucial to creating a compelling vision and engaging others around it. In contrast, teams with low levels of goal clarity and commitment usually perform poorly because members may lose track of (or not be clear about) competing priorities; they may waste their efforts exploring less promising ideas; or they may simply collaborate less effectively because they are not focusing on achieving the same goals. Most of us have seen this in our careers, and many have even experienced working in an organization where clarity was, and probably still is, lacking.

Clarity also contributes to employee job satisfaction. All employees need to know where the organization is going and what their specific role is in the effort to get there. Each person must also understand how that role is an important part of the organization's overall vision and story, in addition to how the role interacts with other team member roles. This understanding of each other's roles affects the attitudes of team members toward the team. It increases cohesiveness and collective orientation, and it promotes autonomy, ownership, job satisfaction, self-accountability, and commitment toward the project, organization, and team success (Braun and Avital 2007).

Clearly, the benefits of role clarity are huge. They have a significant and positive effect on issues as varied and vital as enhancing organizational commitment, reducing job-related tension, lowering burnout, lowering staff turnover, strengthening satisfaction with coworkers, and—perhaps most significantly—maximizing employee performance.

BUILD CONNECTIVITY

Clarity then takes us one step closer to connectivity. Building connectivity means creating an emotional connection with the vision for employees— more specifically, creating that emotional connection for each employee as an individual, so he or she understands how to be a part of making the vision come to pass. If an organization's leaders can help employees connect their hearts to a vision, then the job takes on new meaning and commitment to the organization increases as a result. Connectivity is the glue that ties the intangible and invisible vision to the employees and their actions.

Connectivity is the glue that ties the intangible and invisible vision to the employees and their actions.

In the related research, this connectivity is termed *organizational commitment,* or *OC,* and is defined as the degree of an individual's relations and experiences as a sense of loyalty toward the organization. It encompasses an individual's willingness to extend effort in order to further an organization's goals (Mowday, Steers, and Porter 1979). Measures for organizational commitment often include surveys of employee engagement, employee satisfaction, and employee effectiveness.

With the demographic shift, our employee composition is changing fast, and the emerging workforce requires much greater connectedness. People from Generation Y want to do something that is meaningful to them. If the company doesn't have an altruistic bone, it isn't going to attract this emerging workforce. If it isn't flexible enough to allow them to have a say, they aren't coming.

If you are a traditional leader, you may be thinking, So what? I'll hire someone else. But think again. A recent study highlighted in *Journal of Property Management* indicates that only 7 percent of Gen Y work for Fortune 500 companies, due to the increased interest within this demographic for start-up companies. After reminding readers how large this group is, the article goes on to state that if large corporations want to remain competitive, they must aggressively recruit this demographic— a group that will make up 75 percent of the global workforce by 2025 ("Generation Y: Entrepreneur" 2012).

Some organizations have already started to respond. In 2016, KPMG announced that it was revolutionizing its approach to graduate recruitment. Simon Collins, chairman of KPMG U.K., described this group as "no longer feeling the need to play it safe." He noted that "most are now equally happy to work for a start-up or tech firm as they are a large traditional employer. We are competing with the full gamut for the best brains and talent leaving university: getting our graduate recruitment right is crucial to the long term success of our business" ("KPMG Revolutionises" 2016).

Organizations simply do not have the luxury of saying, "We will just hire someone else," especially if they want to compete for top talent in a fiercely competitive market. Connectedness is valued by all generations, but it's a vital requirement for the fast-emerging Gen Y.

SHAPE CULTURE

A recent headline in *Insigniam Quarterly* read "Culture Eats Everything for Breakfast, Lunch and Dinner" (Bina 2016, 1). That about sums it up. One of the CEO's most important responsibilities is defining and developing a strong culture that supports the company's vision and strategy.

There are many, many definitions of organizational culture. It can be defined as how an organization goes about meeting its goals and missions, how it solves problems, or simply as a deeply rooted value that shapes the behavior of the individuals within the group. In reality, organizational culture is all of these things. It consists of an organization's shared values, symbols, behaviors, and assumptions. Simply put, organizational culture is "the way we do things around here" (Martin 2006).

One of the most relevant definitions of culture is provided by Edgar Schein (1992), who describes it as "the pattern of shared basic assumptions that the group learned as it solved its problems, that has worked well enough to be considered valid, and is passed on to new members as the correct way to perceive, think, and feel in relation to those problems" (9). In other words, it is a product of joint learning, of shared experience. Culture both shapes and is shaped by the accepted behaviors of others: it is mutually reinforcing.

I have worked with incoming leaders who at first see the organization's culture as something they stepped into and must adjust to, and that's true in part. But leaders can—and often need to—shape culture, especially during times of change, and all compelling visions require change and adjustments in the culture. Changing a culture is not easy or quick, but it is worthwhile. It helps to look three or more years into the future and visualize a picture of what the culture must be in order to achieve the vision, and then to begin the work of shaping the culture to fit the picture.

However, *culture change* may not be the right term. A more appropriate term is probably *culture shaping*. Like pottery sculptors who can take clay and shape and reshape it on the potter's wheel, leaders can take an existing culture and begin to reshape it. Over time, the shape of the culture begins to look different, and it takes on the shape that helps achieve the clearly communicated vision, much as the picture in the mind of sculptors helps them mold the clay on the wheel.

Leadership plays a core role in shaping the culture. For example, in a recent study of organizational change in the United States Federal Civil Service, J. T. Hennessey (1998) said that "leadership played a major role in nurturing the appropriate organizational culture which helped to improve the implementation of specific government reforms" (527). Hennessey further argued that "the most effective leaders foster, support, and sustain organizational cultures that facilitate the type of management reform envisioned by 'reinventing government' and the attendant increases in effectiveness and efficiency" (529).

An organization's culture has a substantial impact on its ability to reach its vision, execute its strategy, and achieve business goals and objectives. In fact, if a culture and work environment are cultivated intentionally, it improves an organization's ability to deliver and often helps it become a better place to work. In this way, a strong culture does double duty. It can eliminate the need for detailed instructions or long meetings to discuss how to approach particular issues or problems, and it reduces the level of ambiguity and misunderstanding between functions and departments. The stronger the culture is (assuming it is the right one), the better it is for everyone.

Culture is shaped and defined by a complicated, shifting mesh of many different artifacts, beliefs, values, experiences, and assumptions, and it is worth understanding the different levels at which culture operates.

Artifacts are the visible structures and processes of an organization. They include language, technology, products, dress code, ways to address people, rituals, and ceremonies. They are easy to see but are only meaningful relative to the values and assumptions of the organization.

Espoused beliefs and values are the views that appear and are discussed and which in time come to be the way an organization justifies what it does. In time they become accepted rules. Typically, when a team or group is faced with a new task or challenge, it takes action based on an individual's or subgroup's proposed approach, which in turn is based on assumptions about what will work and what is right or wrong. Once the group observes the plan working or failing, the perception is mentally transformed into a shared belief, and this then becomes a shared assumption. Social validation means that certain values are confirmed by shared experience, which in turn affects how comfortable and free of anxiety members are when they adhere to the new rules. At a very simple level, there are organizations that will buy cupcakes for a team when it is someone's birthday, but it's not a written rule; it is part of the culture that everybody believes in.

This level of culture also includes beliefs and ethical rules that are copied from other places or people and that are explicitly referred to. They are often used as a guide for dealing with situations and for initiating new people on how to behave. Espoused values are therefore useful for coping with uncertainty and events that cannot be controlled. They refer to what people say they do, as opposed to what they may actually do in a given situation.

Basic underlying assumptions are the unconscious beliefs, perceptions, thoughts, and feelings that serve as the ultimate guide to our actions. And because these assumptions are not always confronted or discussed, they can be extremely difficult to change.

These *underlying assumptions* in the culture are important and powerful, because people need stability, and any challenge of a basic assumption will release anxiety and defensiveness. Many organizational change programs fail for that reason, and many individuals fail to adapt or flex their style appropriately for the same reason.

To change requires relearning and readjusting our understanding. This is difficult because questioning our assumptions upsets the stability of our mental and interpersonal worlds, causing anxiety. To avoid anxiety, people want to see that things fit their existing assumptions; and they even do this to the point that they will distort or deny what is really happening. What is needed therefore is leadership that is reassuring, open, and at the same time able to encourage questioning. An approach to leadership that emphasizes both support and challenge is an effective way to help people move their thinking, and moving their thinking is going to be necessary if a leader wants to shape a culture.

So far our analysis and interpretation of the data showed a disconnect between what organizations needed from their leaders and the actual priorities they were being tasked with. While certainly not for the first time in corporate history, organizations were losing sight of their long-term goals and were instead channeling their energy into short-term gains. Unfortunately, with this approach, those who focus on the urgent versus the important soon run out of "quick wins," and once that happens they lose traction and start going backward very quickly.

Just about every organization around the globe is now in a perpetual state of evolution: adapting to market forces, technology, new competitors, and the demands of their customers. In their book *Karaoke Capitalism*, Jonas Ridderstråle,and Kjell Nordström (2004) describe the importance of innovation and differentiation in a world where every idea, product, and service can be copied within days, weeks, and months. But you can't copy a feeling, or a culture, or a sense of being connected to a purpose; you can't copy enthusiasm, energy, passion, and drive. These are at the heart of leading with vision. In the following chapters, we will share a further breakdown and better understanding of each of the four leadership issues—courage, clarity, connectedness, and culture. As we explore each element in greater depth, we will demonstrate what each one looks like in practice with examples of real and current stories that show how the leaders involved were able to make leading with vision a reality.

TAKEAWAYS FROM CHAPTER 4

- How do the EDA *Trends* compare with your own organization?
- How important is the need for your leaders to create a compelling vision and engage others around it?
- What measures do you have in place to determine how engaged your employees are and their level of understanding regarding the vision?

- To what extent is your own existing and future workforce reliant on Generation Y?
- Speak to your Gen Y employees; how do they feel about your organization, where it's going, and their place in it?

CHAPTER 5

Embody Courage

As we continue to dig deeper and comprehend, in detail, *what* it means to effectively engage everyone in the workforce around a vision and *who* is doing this successfully, we turn our focus to courage and its impact on vision. Remembering that courage is twofold—the courage to be bold and the courage to be vulnerable—we will explore in this chapter leaders who embody courage in their organization.

Our first company that embodies courage in boldness demonstrated perseverance, particularly in the relentless pursuit of an idea in spite of significant resistance and difficulties. It is a software start-up in Switzerland that intends to disrupt its industry with a new business model.

THE COURAGE TO BE BOLD

We came across the next industry leader after Simon had a problem with his computer and home network and dialed the number of his telecom provider. To get a real person on the line, he had to wait in a queue listening to boring music for more than ten minutes. The person he eventually reached asked a few questions and then transferred him to someone else. That person, who happened to be located in India, advised Simon to set up an appointment with one of their customer service representatives. The representative was not going to be available for five days from the time of the call and only between 8:00 A.M. to noon or 1:00 P.M. to 5:00 P.M. Of course, he wanted his problem fixed right away, and since he works during the day, the timing for the arrival of the representative was less than ideal.

The more Simon tried to discuss a solution that would actually work for him, the more frustrated he grew with this seemingly immovable situation. At one point, he seriously considered switching providers then and there. With no satisfactory resolution, and an agent who was clearly working from a script, Simon hung up. He felt defeated by the system. He was unimpressed and deeply dissatisfied.

Like many customers who have a bad experience, Simon couldn't wait to relay his frustration to anyone who would listen. Eventually, he told his sad telecom story to his neighbor Mike, who lives on the same floor. Mike said, "Ah, I have a solution for you. My friend Eddie is a very savvy technology guy. He helps me with all kind of topics, from computer backups and music list arrangement to TV and networking configuration."

Simon followed Mike's lead and gave Eddie a call. Sure enough, Eddie arranged to visit at a time that was convenient for Simon, and the problem was soon fixed. Eddie works for Coresystems, an organization that had made some bold moves to provide solutions for people like Simon who were experiencing technology woes and where onsite service was needed. Coresystems had figured out a way to address this common problem with home technology. Their solutions were customer-centric, empowering, and brilliant.

BETTER, FASTER CUSTOMER SERVICE—IN REAL TIME

In an interview with Manuel Grenacher, the CEO of Coresystems, Simon learned that Manuel studied computer science at University of Applied Sciences and Arts Northwestern Switzerland. He started a company to make money so that he could afford to continue his studies. In his last year at the university, he had ten employees writing code and building software for companies.

People who meet Manuel immediately get the impression that he is not your average guy. In fact, Manuel is the type of person who is constantly "looking up"—scanning the corporate horizon and searching for opportunities. Shortly after graduating, he realized that the existing approach to on-site customer service was inadequate for the needs of most people, particularly businesspeople. Technology is now so pervasive that there is almost no aspect of our life, at work or home, that isn't impacted when the technology fails. And when it fails, we want it fixed, and we want it fixed right now. Manuel was aware of plenty of enterprise application platform software products but no real solutions for providing fast and user-friendly customer service. So he decided to create the solution. And with that, he created a new market.

He named the company Coresystems and created a vision to be the leading field-based technical customer service organization. He wanted the company to achieve this by making customer service faster, more real-time, and friendlier. He soon found out that the bar for this was fairly low. In fact, the more Manuel and his team worked in the space, the more they discovered that companies, especially large ones in the technology field, provide really poor customer service.

As technology becomes more complex, and services and product ranges widen, it's really no wonder that telecommunication providers are struggling with customer satisfaction. A Verint Systems study shows that 64 percent of telecom customers experience bad customer service, because the companies are taking too long to resolve problems ("Verint-Commissioned Research" 2013). Based on a 2013 Forrester Research Customer Experience Index across the United Kingdom, France, and Germany, the data shows the dimensions of poor customer service:

- Only 3 percent of companies provide excellent customer service.
- About 57 percent is OK or good.
- 40 percent is poor or very poor (Verint 2013).

It's roughly the same picture for the United States. The 2015 American Customer Satisfaction Index ranked the communications sector—which includes wireless carriers, internet service providers, and cable companies—as the second-worst-performing industry for customer happiness (American Customer Satisfaction Survey 2015).

Manuel and his team believed that they could find a way to solve this problem with better technology and a new operating model. All of this was happening at about the same time as the first iPhone launch in 2007. The use of smartphones and growing empowerment of mobility opened up new possibilities for Coresystems and their big vision. In 2008, Coresystems started building a customer service platform that was fully cloud based.

Manuel recalled those early days thoughtfully. "We even developed a slogan: 'We make core moments, because customer service should be a core moment.' After all, customer service is one of the few remaining competitive differentiators. Price and product options are often so close from one company to another that it doesn't make a difference, but customer service can still set companies apart. Our customer service solution is uniquely geared toward the automation and optimization of field service fleets. We started with an idea that became a vision, and today Coresystems employs 160 people across the globe, utilizes 150,000 field service representatives, and provides customer service for over 7,000 companies."

This incredible journey from nothing to a global business just trips off the tongue for Manuel, but it took courage first to think that the big established players weren't doing all that was possible and then to create a market with a solution that demonstrated how customer service could be done in a new way. It was bold.

CROWDSOURCE CUSTOMER SERVICE

Manuel and his team studied the landscape and found that the biggest barrier to providing excellent customer service was to have the right person available with the right skills at the right time, in the right location. This was especially challenging for geographically dispersed companies with field service representatives, because to hire an adequate number of people and have them on call in case something happens is very expensive. A major trend across all sectors over the last ten years has been for large companies to reduce the cost of delivering customer service by moving call centers to places like India, the Philippines, Thailand, and other countries, where the cost of labor is cheaper. While operating costs come down, the consequence of this type of arrangement is that service levels drop and become ineffective, which is reflected in the low customer satisfaction data stated earlier.

During the interview, Manuel compared his approach to Uber. Uber doesn't employ drivers or own cars. Instead, they crowdsource them, which saves a lot of money. They let people join their network to deliver a driving service. Then they add on a really cool and efficient user experience for the person who needs a ride.

Manuel explained, "We noted the signals for a trend of more shared resources and the fact that the global economic turbulence was having a huge impact on customer service. To take it further, companies didn't have to have their own employees anymore. They could use shared resources such as on-demand workers. It's a crowd-sourced business model. We built on this idea. We decided to have only a few employees to run the core of the business and then use local people to do the on-site work. We needed to find them and ensure they had the right skills, but we didn't need to make them employees. It would be like project work, contract work, temporary work, and they would be free to do other work with other companies or on their own. It is a huge change in the entire field service industry. Like Uber, it's a disruptive change."

CONVINCING A LARGE COMPANY TO ADOPT A NEW BUSINESS MODEL

Manuel knew that this approach was potentially game changing for any business that needed to deliver technical customer service, but, like a compelling vision, he had to bring it to life if he was going to convince big national and multinational businesses to buy into it. He needed to be able to describe and articulate the difference that he could make.

He explained, "If a customer calls in today at Telco Systems, usually he or she will need to wait a week until a technician can come, and then the customer will need to arrange to be at home during whatever time the technician slotted for the service. If the customer has a job and can't be available at the designated time slot, then that is the customer's problem to solve. We wanted to create a service where a customer could call and a representative would come the same day, ideally within three hours. This is the change we wanted to make. We did not believe it was a people issue. There are people in every community who can do the work. Rather, we believed it was a logistics issue and one that we could solve with technology."

With absolute clarity about what he wanted to achieve, Manuel and his team set about developing a product called Mila, which they were able to pilot with Swisscom, the largest telecom company in Switzerland. Manuel said, "We built a network that we called Swisscom Friends. They are tech-savvy individuals, not Swisscom employees, but people who have the skills and knowledge to help customers install, problem-solve, or fix their TVs, iPhones, computers, home networks, wireless routers, and the like."

The people who join and become Swisscom Friends are well-trained individuals who are looking to earn some extra cash. As the Coresystems website shows, there is a strong appeal to Generation Y workers and their desire for flexibility in scheduling. The model that Manuel created is really simple. Swisscom Friends decide when they want to work, and they are allowed to choose which orders to accept. They can choose to be available in the morning, in the evening, or even on a Saturday. Mila, the Coresystems technology platform, is then the go-between for support requests from Swisscom customers. Mila takes a customer request and transmits it to a Friend by e-mail and mobile application. The requests show up for the Friend in the form of service packages or on an hourly basis.

This is a model of working where technology is actually empowering people. Not only is it much more convenient for the customer, it is also less expensive for Swisscom and a much more compelling way to connect those doing the work to the company and its vision for great customer service. Like Uber and other similar platforms, it encourages social interaction. Because customers and Friends live in the same neighborhood, they immediately have something in common and experiences to share. Swisscom is a large national company, but with the help of Mila, it is operating at a very local level.

One of the unexpected benefits that Manuel discovered was that the Friends take more time to solve the customer's problems and needs, even if those needs are not on the original request. When Swisscom employee technicians visit a customer's home, they usually perform one task. If the customer calls because the router doesn't work, the employee technician comes and fixes the router and then needs to get to the next customer. A Friend (who represents Swisscom but is not an employee), on the other hand, can spend more time with the customer answering questions and building a relationship. If a customer says, "Hey, by the way, how does this Dropbox app work?" a Friend will most likely take the time to show the customer, whereas an employee technician will often need to get to the next appointment.

"We wanted to make a move and do something new in the industry. We are completely changing the field services business model."

Manuel's courage to be bold and reimagine the service delivery model has resulted in multiple benefits. "First, it builds community within the neighborhood," Manuel said. "Second, there are minimal or no travel costs because the Friends can just walk over to help since they are local, and third the Swisscom Friend explains things or solves the problem from a user-experience point of view, not from a technical background. With our crowd-sourced approach there is flexibility. And financially, it makes sense for everyone. Swisscom saves money, the customer pays less, and the Swisscom Friend makes an income. Everyone wins."

As Manuel noted, with the crowdsource field service model, Coresystems builds a local community of technicians who are geographically closer to the customers. It turns out that the customers don't care if the people Swisscom sends are employees or contractors; for them it's only important that they get their problems fixed quickly and conveniently. Customer experience is paramount in every competitive industry, so those businesses using the Coresystems model to deliver technical service to their customers are not only able to reduce their costs; they also have a differentiator, which gives them a competitive advantage.

There is one more additional benefit, which Manuel explained. "With the richness of data we collect using our technology platform, we can use a range of data points to best match customers and technicians. We don't have to be limited to geography; we can match people by language, for example."

Speaking of the telecom world in general, between 40 percent and 64 percent of customers state how unhappy they are with the level of customer service they receive. Consequently, we can expect that quite a few people actually cancel their contracts and go elsewhere. In contrast, Coresystems' technology is helping to create better personal experiences, which leads to higher customer satisfaction scores and ultimately to more customer loyalty.

Coresystems now has more people in the field than Swisscom itself, with more than 2,000 Friends already and about a hundred joining every month. The more Friends in the service field, the easier it is to match the right Friend with the customer and provide faster and better service.

A BOLD START

Manuel started with an idea and a vision to deliver better customer service in real time. He said, "I wanted to try out the idea, but it was a really costly project. Three years ago no one, I mean no one, believed in this idea."

Manuel found that it was very hard to convince people that his vision of a different model would work. People simply couldn't imagine that there would be a more effective or efficient way of working than what they already had. In the face of such negativity, it takes a courageous leader to continue, but Manuel always had a compelling vision, which is what drove him and his team. And—as is the case with most success stories—he also caught a few breaks along the way.

Manuel said, "I needed a big player like Swisscom to create big news."

Initially, he met with much resistance. Three years ago they said things like, "Oh, no, we have our professional service," and, "Why should we do this?" It was unbelievably challenging. Manuel talked to many people about the vision, pitching the idea relentlessly. With all of his influencing skills, he finally convinced Swisscom to run a pilot. They started in the city of Zurich with only 200 Friends. Next they collected all of the important data points and built a chart with key performance indicators for feedback from the very first customer experiences. They sent that data to the CEO of Swisscom, and it allowed the Swisscom leaders to see, in a measurable way, that the customers were really happy. Swisscom fell in love with the idea. It was a big moment.

> *"We had to fight for the vision. Today it's much easier because the numbers tell a great story, but in the beginning, we had to fight for it."*
>
> —Manuel Grenacher

The idea would have died if Manuel and his team hadn't been relentless in their pursuit. They understood that the idea was new and different, which can sometimes be very uncomfortable. People can be afraid of change even when they need it. It requires them to be bold as well. The vision was clear to Manuel; it was even clear to Swisscom, but they just didn't believe in it until they saw the data. Through the pilots, Manuel's team learned to go out really quickly, test the technology, innovate, make small sprints, have more pilots, get feedback, make tweaks, and then do it all again. Doing small, fast implementation steps worked, and it wasn't long before the vision became a reality.

Today, it's much easier because the numbers tell a great story. Coresystems has a significantly higher Net Promoter Score (NPS) than Swisscom itself, indicating that the customer service they provide is much better than the traditional service. It isn't because the people are better; the main differentiators are the convenience of the delivery and the fact that customers can have their issues solved faster.

GAME CHANGER

Today, many companies, in industries across the board, are ramping up real-time service options. Given that people are now used to getting everything from car rides to groceries on demand, retailers like Amazon are offering real-time customer service that delivers packages not just in the same day but also as soon in that day as possible.

Coresystems believes that if the trend continues, and it is very likely to, customers will expect service technicians to come within one or two hours. In anticipation, Manuel is building on his original bold vision and is now developing an app that will deliver service as quickly as Uber delivers cars to its customers. With an ever-increasing number of people joining the service network of Friends, it will be possible to deliver service faster than ever. Coresystems is always evolving the technology to improve the experience for technicians and customers, and they are using skills, age, time, and geographic criteria to decide the match that will deliver the highest level of service for the customer. "Intelligent matching is the future," Manuel stated, "and that future is almost here."

ORGANIC FRUIT IN THE RECYCLED LUNCH BAG

In another great example of leadership that embodies courage, Simon found Jimbo's...Naturally!, a small grocery store chain with five stores in San Diego County. He visited their store in Carmel County, which is also where their head office is housed. There he saw well-presented merchandise and, at the cashier's desk, the company's vision statement, which covers the wall: "*A piece of organic fruit in every child's recycled lunch bag.*" It is a bold vision statement and a great example of making the vision visual. People can see it; it paints a picture. It's compelling, and it's something with which both employees and customers can connect.

The Jimbo's vision is a reflection of the company founder's dedication to natural and organic food over the last forty years. Jim "Jimbo" Someck is a man who truly practices what he preaches. He is fully committed to protecting the environment for future generations and encouraging a healthy lifestyle for everyone. As an avid runner and strict vegetarian, he strongly believes in healthy nutrition that contains organic ingredients whenever possible, no white sugar, no harmful chemicals, and no pre-servatives. His family practices what he preaches; they have daily family meals, which they prepare with fresh ingredients and make from scratch.

In 1973, after his studies at Cornell University in New York, Jim trav-eled across the United States to visit his brother in San Diego. He volun-teered for a cooperative, with the aim to distribute affordable food from local farmers to consumers. In 1984 he started in the health food business in a job that involved breaking down cardboard boxes. Through these experiences, Jim developed a passion to provide the highest quality of organic and natural food, which became the mission of his business.

To achieve his ambitious mission, Jim wanted to establish clarity from the outset and create the right ethos, so he sat down and composed a Bill of Rights. His bill described, in simple language, how the business would operate and its role in the local community ("The Jimbo's Ethos" 2016).

One key element of their ethos is not to allow artificial ingredients in their products. Jim has remained true to this conviction even when suppliers of products with GMO ingredients warned him that he would lose customers if he didn't carry their products. Jim told them that he was willing to take that risk if it meant standing by his principles (Mercola 2012). Over time, he realized that while he did actually lose a few cli-ents, he gained many more because they valued his principles and trusted his brand.

Jim's stance against the use of GMO ingredients in products is further evidence of his boldness as a leader, and it has resulted in major manufac-turers changing their own policies. Jim said, "Our buyers have persuaded several manufacturers, including Endangered Species, Angie's Kettlecorn, Popcorn Indiana, Turtle Island (Tofurkey) and Sunfood Superfoods to switch out suspect ingredients for GMO-free ingredients, and whenever possible, organic ingredients."

I believe in working cooperatively with manufacturers to go GMO-free. But we also let manufacturers know that we will eventually replace their products with GMO-free alternatives if they do not have a plan for removing GMO ingredients. Our buyers meet with manufacturers and brokers, who now understand our position and don't offer us GMO foods. Our stance on GMOs has led several manufacturers to enroll in the Non-GMO Project in order to keep us as a customer" (Organic Retail and Consumer Alliance 2013).

Today, the Jimbo's vision is a reality, with a $10 million business and five stores, and thanks to the bold determination of its leader, Jimbo's is punching well above its weight.

Jim knows that his unwavering view of GMO has created a loyal customer base, and he also understands the need for absolute clarity with his staff and customers. He said, "It's important to be clear with store staff about why non-GMO policies are being adopted, so that the staff can communicate more knowledgeably with customers. It's also important to communicate a clear policy to your customers. We notify our customers when we plan to discontinue at-risk brands. Retailing involves a delicate balance between wanting to do what is right and best for the industry and providing customers with what they want. If you educate your consumers, help them understand your policies and decisions, they will support you. ("Jimbo's…Naturally!" 2013).

In an additional step to his vision, in 2008 Jimbo's stopped providing customers with plastic bags. This wasn't about saving money; he wanted to encourage customers to recycle the bags they already had so that together they would generate less waste. As an incentive, every customer who brings in a reusable bag receives credit via a wooden nickel, and all proceeds from the wooden nickels go to local nonprofits. Bringing your own bag to Jimbo's means you're contributing to a good cause.

"Doing the right thing, regardless of the impact on our bottom line" is Jim's philosophy on leadership. "We've found that if we take care of our employees, they will take care of our customers. ("Jimbo's…Naturally!" 2013).

The bold vision of this small company is paying off. Jim's years of hard work and commitment to his customers, employees, community, and the environment were nationally recognized in 1995 when Jimbo's... Naturally! was awarded Store of the Year by *Health Food Business* magazine. In June of 2012, Jimbo's received two prestigious industry awards: Socially Responsible Retailer of the Year and *Whole Foods* magazine Retailer of the Year. Today Jimbo's serves as the innovator and is in the forefront when it comes to natural and organic food. In fact, more than 95 percent of all products at Jimbo's are organic, compared to about 50 percent in Whole Foods stores.

THE COURAGE TO BE VULNERABLE

While having a bold vision is exciting, it doesn't mean that it automatically takes off. In fact, as we studied bold visions and how they started, we realized that the bolder the vision, the harder it may be initially to get others to come along. But on the good side, a little bit of success can breed more success. It causes others to quickly jump in when they see that the spark of an idea has real possibilities of becoming a flame.

It takes boldness to advance an idea from inception to product through to market success and revenue generation, just as Manuel Grenacher has displayed with Coresystems and Jim Someck did with Jimbo's. However, as we discussed before, courage, when it comes to vision, is twofold: the courage to be bold and the courage to be vulnerable.

The courage to be vulnerable is much more of a personal issue. Looking into it further, the word *vulnerable* has its roots in Latin and means exposed to the things that hurt, physically or emotionally.

Being vulnerable means showing up and letting ourselves be seen, with all the imperfections of being human. That is exactly what makes vulnerability difficult. Sometimes we just don't want to put ourselves out there. Human beings are not perfect; we all make mistakes. Sometimes we fail or we mess up, or our thoughts become paralyzed in the moment. Admitting those failures and stumbles to others can be difficult, terrifying, and dangerous, and it takes courage.

We often see leaders struggle with being vulnerable. They are leaders, after all, and they do not want to appear weak. However, the difference between being weak and being vulnerable is courage, and to see vulnerability as a weakness is a weakness in itself. A weak leader can never truly be strong, whereas a leader who is willing to be vulnerable can be strong and powerful.

As my coauthors and I thought about this defining attribute of good leadership, we sought examples of vulnerability coming from a place of inner strength. We wanted to demonstrate how a leader's willingness to be vulnerable can have a real impact on others and how it beckons those people to become fully engaged around a shared vision.

A VISION FOR SAFETY AND A DANCE

Todd Bastean and his colleagues are an example of such courage in both boldness and vulnerability. Todd is the CEO of Bunge North America (BNA), one of the largest business units of Bunge Limited, a global agribusiness and food ingredient company dedicated to improving the global food supply chain. It was founded in 1818 in Amsterdam and has since had headquarters in five different countries across three continents. Today, Bunge operates in over 40 nations with over 35,000 colleagues.

> "**Courage** is not the absence of fear. It is acting in spite of it."
>
> —Mark Twain

Todd progressed from CFO of BNA to the role of CEO in June of 2013. From the moment he became CEO, Todd and his senior team were courageous, moving swiftly to make bold changes in leadership, acquisitions, divestitures, and a large-scale reorganization. Their strength as a team under Todd's leadership was both surprising and exciting for those who worked at Bunge, but Todd's personal leadership began to shine brightest in his courage to be vulnerable.

The word *courage* actually comes from a French word, *curage*, which means *heart* and *innermost feelings*. It is a common metaphor for inner strength. The difference between Todd and many leaders that we've come across is that Todd is willing to acknowledge his own strengths and weaknesses. He shows the courage to be vulnerable by taking risks emotionally. He never tries to hide his caring nature. Under Todd's leadership, BNA has significantly increased benefits that contribute to a better work-life balance for all colleagues. Personally, he gives hugs, sends gifts, and calls people when he is aware that someone has concerns or issues at work or at home. He invites young colleagues in the organization to meetings and to plant visits so they can get to know and learn from each other. People who spend very much time with Todd will see him shed a tear or get choked up when he talks about his Bunge colleagues. Here are two specific examples where Todd's courage through vulnerability were particularly inspiring.

Zero-Incident Safety Culture

The first example is based on Todd's vision for safety. While the organization already had a mandate for high safety standards and a zero-incident safety culture, his focus on safety is rooted in a very personal situation. When Todd was a child, his uncle, a man he was very close to, was killed in an industrial accident at work. Todd remembers that day vividly, particularly the impact that the news brought to his entire family and the lives that were forever changed.

Todd shares this story when he talks to his Bunge colleagues about safety. He mentions how much his aunt misses her husband, how much his cousins miss their father, and how much he misses his uncle's smile. Even though sharing this story is part of his personal pain, Todd is willing to be vulnerable in the hope that it will help even one more person to share his passion and vision for safety.

When Todd learns of others around the globe who are impacted by a safety incident, he feels as if he owns it. In an interview, Todd said, "I feel as though—and I actually am—just as responsible as if they were in our part of the organization. As a senior executive leader in our organization, I feel it is absolutely just as much my responsibility. I wonder how we, even from North America, could have helped more to prevent such a tragedy. When there is a death somewhere across the globe, we do stand-downs and when we do, I can never get through them without choking up. I know what our colleague's family and friends are going through."

Todd and his senior team didn't hold back on safety. Together they established the vision they felt was right for BNA: Zero incidents throughout the organization—nothing, nada, not one incident would be tolerable. They believe it is achievable. Together they work diligently to ensure that every colleague goes home safely to his or her family every day.

Tactically, the BNA team is doing all of the normal safety initiatives, such as oversight through key leadership positions reporting to the CEO and other senior leaders, all kinds of detail work programs, plus sharing of best practices and personal stories. Then, globally they do more by adding important pieces, such as tools that can be leveraged and used across the world to give plant managers and other leaders what they need to take care of their teams around hazardous energy, falls from heights, confined spaces, hoisted loads, and mobile equipment, to name a few. All of this effort is great, and yet it is, of course, expected in today's work environment from leading organizations around the world. However, what has fundamentally changed in the BNA culture is not the numbers or the tactical initiatives. It's the warmth.

In the last calendar year, BNA had a very successful rollout of a Stand Up for Safety program, with 99.5 percent of colleagues participating. Todd has personally participated in several facilities' rollouts, and he also has reached out personally to BNA facility managers over 100 times in a preceding twelve-month period. He does this annually, speaking to each facility manager about safety, facility activities, culture, and so forth, with the conversations ranging from thirty minutes to over an hour. In that same twelve months, he personally visited twenty-three facilities regarding safety, and again he does this annually, visiting twenty to thirty facilities to touch base, spend some time together with the facility teams, and discuss how they are doing on their safety journey.

A few unique touches that Todd believes have really connected with the BNA colleagues are the handwritten, personal notes on achieving safety milestones and the thoughtful holiday cards that he writes to the facilities. In addition, all BNA senior leaders also take their time to go to the facilities to talk about safety, to learn, and to share. The colleagues at the facilities are incredibly proud of who they are and what they do, and the BNA leaders relish the opportunities to put down their phones, set aside their email, and just listen and learn from those closest to the work.

Todd also initiated a "meet and greet" so that three to four times per year, the BNA leaders meet and greet the colleagues as they arrive at work. They smile, welcome them to work, and then share a little safety message, such as, "Please be sure to use the handrails on the stairs." It's just another way to show that every colleague is cared for.

We judge ourselves by our intentions. We are judged by our behaviors.

Todd and his team are out front on the vision for safety, and their personal touches continually build the BNA safety culture. The dividends are high. The numbers are showing great progress: lost-time injuries are down approximately 50 percent, and total recordable incidents are down between 20 and 30 percent. But it's the softer side that Todd likes to talk about. He and others on the senior team are often approached by BNA colleagues they do not know well or have never met. These colleagues thank them, some with tears in their eyes, for what the BNA leaders are doing around safety. The BNA colleagues feel it, and they tell stories of how it is impacting the way they think about safety not only at work but also at home. A BNA colleague who is retiring after seventeen years recently sent Todd a note that gives yet another voice to their progress toward his vision. She said,

> I want to thank each of you for the opportunity to work for a company as high-caliber as Bunge is! . . . One thing I am really taking with me as I leave is the attitude toward safety—and that comes directly from this culture. . . . I think we so have it right in this office and with these people. It just spills over into your private life and that is a good thing.

Dancing with the St. Louis Stars

Another time that Todd set an example of leading with courage through vulnerability was when he participated in Dancing with the St. Louis Stars.[1] This is an event in St. Louis where some of the most notable leaders in the city compete in a dance competition to raise money for the Independence Center, an organization committed to providing a comprehensive system of high-quality programs and services for adults in the St. Louis metropolitan area with serious and persistent mental illnesses so they can live and work in the community independently and with dignity. The winner is determined not by the greatest dance, though many of them are very good, but by which team raises the most money.

When Todd accepted the call to participate with a dance partner, professional instructor Lucy Fitzgerald, he decided to do more than put in his time. He wanted to win, to have fun, and to be different. And he did just that. Their performance was so fun it brought down the house! As the performance video of Todd and Lucy shows (*https://youtu.be/7lMMVSDAJH4*), he was clearly willing to take a chance. Todd is not a professional dancer, but his performance was real, vulnerable, human, and courageous. He didn't care what others thought.

Because of Todd's willingness to be vulnerable, his colleagues and many of BNA's business partners came to the table with their time, their support, and their checkbooks to support an important part of the community in which they serve. Todd and Lucy ultimately raised more than $250,000 for the center. How often do CEOs avoid doing something new or different because they are afraid to look weak when, in fact, doing something like this may be the very thing that connects them with their teams?

"C'est le ton qui fait la musique."
(It's the tone that makes the music.)

---

[1] For more information about Dancing with the St. Louis Stars, see *www.dancingwiththestlouisstars.org*.

Social researcher and shame expert Brené Brown (2012) sums it up this way: "Vulnerability is not weakness. It is basically uncertainty, risk, and emotional exposure. Our only choice is a question of engagement. Our willingness to own and engage with our vulnerability determines the depth of our courage and the clarity of our purpose; the level to which we protect ourselves from being vulnerable is a measure of our fear and disconnection" (2). The vulnerability has to come from the heart. It can't be staged. People are very good at detecting a fake. If the leader isn't really running a risk of getting hurt, then the vulnerability isn't real and it won't connect with people.

There is a key principle in leadership: It's not the intention that counts; the behaviors leaders demonstrate every day are what build trust and credibility with our constituencies. Manuel, Jim, and Todd didn't just think about bringing others along; they acted, and they influenced others with their leadership style and convincing narratives. They put themselves out there in a way that could have attracted derision and criticism but instead won them respect and loyalty.

Manuel had a vision for a better way to deliver technical service in the field, and despite two years of rejections he continued to believe in the idea and work toward the vision. Furthermore, he convinced others to believe in it too. Today his team is relentlessly pursuing new goals. As the Coresystems website declares, "We are on a mission to make field service more efficient and satisfying," and Manuel is right there, leading from the front.

Jim has created a vision that is inspiring for both staff and customers. Like Todd's approach with BNA, Jim has allowed his personal principles and beliefs to set the agenda for Jimbo's, and this approach has won him respect, loyalty, and industry acclaim.

Leading with courage requires looking into the mirror, thinking about how others are impacted, and considering how others experience your behaviors. Ultimately, it's not the content that makes employees charged and motivated, it's how you go about engaging them. In French there is a famous saying: *"C'est le ton qui fait la musique"*—It's the tone that makes the music ("French" 2016). This also applies to leadership. It's not just the words; it's the feeling that you put into them that will resonate with your teams and establish an emotional connection that will lead to behavioral change and, ultimately, successful outcomes.

Manuel, Jim, and Todd are great leaders. Each man is quite inspiring. However, apart from their courage, they were also very clear about what they wanted to achieve and how to do it. And clarity is what we will learn more about next.

TAKEAWAYS FROM CHAPTER 5

- There are two types of courage: bold and vulnerable. Visionary leaders need to demonstrate both types.
  - When was the last time that you demonstrated an ability to be bold?
  - When was the last time you demonstrated vulnerability to your colleagues?
- Think of a situation where you had to stand firm without appearing reckless:
  - What did you do?
  - How did you handle the situation?
  - What could you have done better?
- When was the last time you used a personal story to get your message across?
- What presentations do you have coming up where a personal message would have more impact?
- Do you role-model the behaviors you want to see in others?
- What three behaviors could you change about yourself to send the right message to your team?

CHAPTER 6

Forge Clarity

IN CHAPTER 4, we described clarity in terms of: clarity of vision, clarity of communication, clarity of roles, clarity of process, and decision-making clarity. Leaders who get this right achieve absolute alignment, from the vision, down through the organization to personal objectives and behaviors, ultimately influencing the way each person makes every decision.

As we went through our data, experiences, and interviews, we found an example in Chris Lofaso, a regional manager for a global technology company, who shared his own experience of trying to achieve clarity throughout his organization. In the recent past, Chris had been promoted from a regional management role to a general management role in his company. He then relocated from San Diego to Northern California, where he was suddenly responsible for leading a $100 million business and 300 people across three locations. He evaluated his new area of responsibility and concluded that there were three areas that required immediate focus:

- Employee engagement, which was low.
- Customer satisfaction levels, which were below targets.
- Profit targets, which were consistently being missed.

Specifically, Chris quickly realized that there was confusion and a lack of clarity regarding the goals of the leadership team as well as individual roles and responsibilities. Without these, no one appeared to be accountable. It also became evident that there was a lack of trust among the leadership team. Silos had been created, and there was no transparency between teams, which was leading to significant inefficiencies. As a result, his organization had missed its financial targets for ten consecutive years.

There were, of course, clear targets and measurements in place for financial results, client satisfaction goals, and employee engagement, but there was no clear plan of how to achieve them and no one was taking responsibility. This general lack of clarity had created a culture of blame, negativity, low morale, and a disengaged staff.

Chris knew that he needed to address these problems as a top priority. The underlying and most critical element to address was the dysfunction of the leadership team. He asked himself three key questions:

1. How do we get the leadership team engaged and aligned?
2. What are we here to accomplish, and what is each person going to contribute?
3. How are we going to do it?

Chris rolled up his sleeves and went to work. Clarity became his mission. He started creating clarity around individual roles and responsibilities, ensuring that everyone understood their responsibilities as well as how their role tied into the overall vision and strategy. He instilled a culture of accountability by establishing measures of success and time lines and then staying close to his team so that they were successful in meeting both. He also created a culture of transparency around expectations so that team members shared their measures and time lines with the other team members, ensuring another level of accountability.

Very quickly, employees at every level began to respond. When people know what is expected of them, they want to deliver; when they know what they are responsible for, they are usually happy to be accountable. Over time, a new culture emerged. Chris felt that chasing the numbers wasn't going to achieve his goal, but by changing the culture and creating clarity for everyone, he knew that if the teams were capable, they would deliver the results. And they did. Two years later, Chris' organization was the only one, out of nineteen peer organizations across the United States, to achieve its profit goal in all three of their product divisions. He attributed that success primarily to their ability to gain clarity around the vision for success—first in the leadership team and then throughout the organization. The sections that follow highlight the steps that Chris actually took.

THREE LEVELS OF CLARITY

Clarity is the thread that starts with your vision and works through every layer of the organization down to the individual daily objective of each member of staff. Leaders who establish a sense of clarity have confidence that no matter what tasks employees are doing, they are working toward the organization's vision.

Chris described clarity as "a state of being that enables alignment and accountability." He said, "When we experience clarity in business at all levels of the organization, everyone goes to work with a laser-like focus every day. They know what to do, how to do it, and the results that will be achieved."

From the research we identified three levels of clarity.

Level One is about creating organizational clarity. This is the first acid test for your vision/mission/purpose. Are the phrases clear, or are they just trendy, generic words of the moment? Do they speak to your employees and help them understand what you want to achieve as an organization? For instance, you can imagine that when Microsoft said it wanted to put a PC in every home running Windows, each team at Microsoft had a conversation about their role in making that happen.

Level Two addresses team and workgroup clarity. This is about clarifying what each team is responsible for delivering collectively and how teams can work together to achieve shared objectives. Each team will have its own roles and responsibilities, and often other teams will be relying on them to play their part. The team is only as strong as the weakest individual, which means that each person has to be accountable.

Level Three provides individual clarity. This specifically speaks to building a common culture at an individual level where each person can answer these questions: What is your role on the team? What are you responsible for accomplishing? Individual clarity ensures that everyone who bounds up the stairs in the morning knows exactly what they are doing and what is expected of them. The clarity around alignment of roles and responsibilities is fundamental to success.

Going back to our Gen Y community for a second, these levels of clarity are precisely what they are looking for in an organization. They want to know where they fit in, what is expected of them, and what goals their work is helping to achieve. Remember Bruce and his experience? What he didn't get was any clarity, so his job felt worthless to him. This led him to find a position where he went to work knowing exactly what he was doing and why. It could be argued that it is easier to provide that kind of clarity within a small smart-up but more difficult in a larger organization, but Chris Lofaso knew that he had to find a way despite having over 300 employees in numerous locations.

Chris realized that while his organization had clear financial targets, they didn't have a clear vision that employees could connect with. Without a well-defined future state and underlying purpose, there were no values that informed how people behaved. This is what had led to the dysfunctionality that started with the leadership team and permeated down throughout the organization. Chris' first job was to work with the leadership team on a purpose that people could get excited about.

Chris gathered his team together and led a workshop that began with four key questions:

1. What gets us out of bed in the morning?
2. What do we want for our organization?
3. What do we want to be famous for?
4. How do we ensure that all individuals know they have a part to play?

After much discussion, revision, and subsequent consultation, this is what they agreed on: *We create customer loyalty and profitably grow our business by empowering our employees with a vision of world-class service.* When they went through the process, they took the time to break down the words *empowering* and *create customer loyalty* in order to establish a common understanding.

Chris said the team came to understand and believe that when they empowered their employees, they would see increased levels of engagement and commitment. They also believed that employee commitment would lead to higher levels of customer service, which would in turn create customer loyalty, leading to profitable growth and ultimately becoming a best-in-class organization. Chris said, "At the end of the day, it doesn't matter what industry you're in, what product you sell, or what company you work for. We are all in the people business."

If organizations take care of their employees, the employees will look after the customers, and the organization will grow in a healthy and profitable way.

CREATE ACCOUNTABILITY FOR RESULTS AND BEHAVIORS

It's impossible to achieve overall clarity without providing accountability for, and creating clarity around, specific goals and expected outcomes. People need to know clearly what you expect of them, as Chris noted and addressed when he took over as general manager. Organizations that take steps to ensure there is clarity help employees understand what they will be held accountable for and how to stay aligned with the organization's purpose. Here are a few steps that help achieve clarity around expectations.

1. **Establish clear and realistic expectations**. Align individual goals with the team goals and ensure that there is a thread back to the organization's overall purpose or vision.

2. **Ensure all goals can be measured**, and monitor progress, providing helpful feedback and addressing issues before they become a problem. Just having a monthly one-on-one meeting with each team member can reveal skill gaps, personal development needs, challenges each individual may be facing. Ultimately, the leader's role is to support the employees' success in their roles.

3. **Clarify the consequences.** Too often when people hear the word *consequences*, they think of punishment, but this is really about helping employees understand their value to the organization. *Consequences* refers to positive reinforcement as well as to corrections. Feedback does both: "Hey, you're doing well." "You're a little off target—what can I help you do to get back on target?" "That's great what you did; let's do more of that." Be less critical about performance and focus on helping employees get an "A" in what they're doing.

Ultimately, creating accountability on a one-to-one level is accomplished through clear expectations, measurements against those expectations, and consistent consequences—both positive and corrective.

APPLY THE CONCEPT OF FOLLOWERSHIP

An old adage notes that a leader without followers is just a lone person. Critical to the success of Chris' organization was his encouragement of strong followership. Chris' experience had taught him that people don't follow a job title; they follow a person. He also knew that the best leaders are those who demonstrate values that others can relate to.

People don't follow a job title; they follow a person.

Chris believes that everyone in a department or team needs to understand a little bit about the leader's history and background, particularly since life experiences (e.g., our parents' approach, socioeconomic factors, mentors we have encountered, etc.) influence us and help shape who we are today, including how we choose what is important and which values we'll embrace. (They also affect which values we'll reject, just as Jim Someck's personal stance against GMOs shaped his business.) If employees are going to follow the leader, they really want to know who that leader is. Otherwise, there's a lack of emotional connection.

The willingness of leaders to share this information also shows the courage of vulnerability, because it's often hard for leaders to open themselves up in such a way with so many people. Personally, Chris likes to share things about where he grew up, briefly discuss how he was raised, and generally show that he is a human being.

TEAM CHARTER, THE "SECRET" WEAPON

Another important piece of clarity is for the team to understand what they can expect from the leader. The leader can role-model behaviors and set their own expectations. Asking the right questions during meetings, requesting certain types of data, and being seen to do things differently can very quickly convey key messages, such as: Here's how I'm going to behave. Here's how I'm going to treat you. Here's the framework and the behavioral norms the team will work within. Here's what I expect you to do as one of the members of my team. I expect punctuality. I expect professionalism. I expect you to treat customers with the ultimate respect, and I expect mutual respect between our team members.

Putting these elements on the table gives the team clarity and allows them to connect with both you and the organization. How often have you heard someone say, "I just don't know where I stand with my boss?" Without clarity, there are no parameters—and without parameters, employees can unintentionally end up doing the wrong thing.

To address this need for clarity, Chris created a team charter. He explained, "We put all of the expectations into a *team charter*. It became the framework of our leadership team and a living, breathing document that we all subscribe to. It spells out our values and supporting behaviors.

We realized that it is easy to state a value, but that value really is meaningless unless you can define—and clarify—what it means from a behavioral standpoint."

For Chris, creating the charter was in itself an exercise in clarity. Chris and his team agreed up front that nothing could be included that couldn't be defined and explained in simple terms. Like many organizations, a core value that Chris and his team identified was "respect for individuals," but Chris pushed his team and wanted to know what that really meant on a daily basis. They started by looking at the exact opposite ("disrespect for individuals") and asking themselves what would happen if people didn't respect individuals? This led to a great discussion, and from that they identified some clear, positive, supporting behaviors that everyone could relate to:

- We respect the diversity of everyone's opinions and values.
- We treat others the way we want to be treated as individuals.
- We're open to other viewpoints without personal bias or judgment.
- We're considerate of others, especially when they're speaking or presenting.
- We seek to understand and listen with open-mindedness.
- We treat our customers and our employees as if our livelihood is solely in their hands.

The great thing about the team charter is that it is completely transparent, and it applies to everyone. If Chris himself should fall short, he would expect someone to pull him up, and as such, he expects all of his team to lead by example.

No organization remains the same for long. Change is now an inevitable part of doing business, so the team charter has to be organic. At least once a quarter, Chris and his team revisit the charter and assess whether it is still fit for purpose, still challenging, and still relevant. Where necessary, they make changes and communicate those changes to the wider team.

The charter has also been integral to the on-boarding process for new employees. Chris explains, "When new employees join our organization,

I sit them down and explain the team charter with them: 'Okay, you're now part of this team. Here's our purpose. Here are our values. Here's how you're expected to behave.' I also have other members of the team meet them to expose them to the values and to give them a different perspective of the values. This accelerates the learning curve for new employees. It gives them a clear and transparent view of our values and norms and immediately provides a common platform for them to engage with the other managers, employees, and business leaders."

The charter is a direct input into the culture. Chris uses it as a quick way to begin to assimilate new employees into their strong culture.

The team charter has come to symbolize everything positive about the organization. It informs the culture and sets the standards by which everyone behaves. Chris says, "One of the most positive outcomes was a significant increase in the level of engagement and commitment by each leader, as well as their respective work groups. People became rejuvenated. They were reenergized, and their level of emotional commitment skyrocketed."

THE MARCH TO BODEGA BAY

In Chris' second year in charge, the teams were close to hitting their targets. It was the first time in ten years, and they were only six months away from success. Chris gathered his team, and together they drew up a plan of action that would guarantee their success. They called it the "March to Bodega Bay." Chris explained, "Bodega Bay was the place in Northern California where we were going to go to celebrate!"

What Chris had created was a short-term vision. It wasn't about hitting the numbers; it was about getting to the party at Bodega Bay.

Progress was tracked each month. Chris said, "And you know what? Each and every time, if there was a shortfall, someone on the leadership team stepped up to make it happen! The emotional commitment and collaboration were incredible."

With that level of commitment, it isn't any wonder that the organization achieved their goals, and at the company annual conference, it was Chris' teams that were recognized and rewarded for their extraordinary efforts.

"Our success as a team touched the very core of who we were."

—Chris Lofaso

He said, "Soon after the awards ceremony, I organized an off-site team strategy retreat—in Bodega Bay, of course. This included a dinner to celebrate our accomplishments from the prior year. It was amazing what I witnessed that evening! Spontaneously, folks began to stand up and reflect upon the past years' experience. The mutual recognition between team members, as well as the emotions that emerged that evening, were incredibly strong. As we circled the table and folks described their appreciation for each other, emotions began to rise. Some folks began to cry. The team had been so emotionally committed to our success and achieved something so special that they were overwhelmed by emotion. Our success as a team touched the very core of who we were. We set a clear goal for ourselves and worked very hard to achieve something very difficult. The satisfaction we experienced was amazing."

Two years earlier, Chris had taken the helm of an underperforming organization, but by creating clarity at every level, for every employee, he had changed the culture and turned the entire scenario into something positive, something meaningful.

CLARITY BEFORE STRATEGY

Forging clarity isn't just for big businesses; in fact it can be just as, if not more, important for small businesses who are running on adrenaline and sheer enthusiasm to be really clear about where they are heading. For example, Simon recently worked with an organization that was still in its infancy. The company provided public relations services and created ads for businesses that were interested in moving into the digital realm.

He met with the two partners, who were seeking some help with their own leadership development and wanted to learn how to manage cultural change in a small but growing business.

Simon found that these partners, like the leaders of many small businesses, were tempted to cover everything and not exclude any possibility for fear of losing out. Since that approach would lead to disaster, the goal became to create some clarity. The more clearly the partners could think about what they did, wanted to do, and wanted to achieve, the easier it would be for them to develop a strategic plan and ultimately understand what sort of organization they needed to create.

Simon helped them develop a list of questions for the partners to answer individually. Then they shared their answers with each other in order to establish whether or not they were thinking along the same lines.

The questions were grouped and relevant to their industry:

- How would you describe the work you do?
- How would your customers describe the work you do for them?
- What are the deliverables that you create for your customers?
- What are customers seeking when they call you?
- What does your ideal customer look like and why?
- What attributes and skills do the people you hire have?
- How would you describe the culture of your business?
- What are your emotional goals as a business?
- What are your financial goals as a business?
- What are your personal goals as leaders?
- What will success look like for you?

From their answers, some common themes and aspirations emerged that would ultimately help form part of a strategy and also help them articulate their business to employees and customers.

Taking the exercise further, the two partners wrote a narrative that described what their business would look like in five years. This was a classic visualization exercise. In a previous chapter, we discussed how

Kristi Overton Johnson could see and feel every curve and bump on her water ski course with absolute clarity during a visualization exercise. In this case, the two partners needed to see the path for their business.

Once completed—and without even realizing it—they had clarified what they wanted the culture to be, the types of clients they wanted to work with, the types of people they would employ, how teams would work together, and how their own roles would impact the success of the business. Here are some of phrases they came up with as they pictured their business five years down the road.

We are a creative agency that supports our clients through advertising, public relations, interactive media, and design.

We have a team of fifty people with offices on the East and West Coasts. Our Los Angeles headquarters is a large and airy loft-style office with high ceilings and lots of windows, located in a funky fun area. The spaces are open and filled with light and laughter—they contain few walls and many seating areas and workstations equipped for multiple uses and work styles. Our offices include comfortable furniture, original art, areas for music, areas for quiet, and meeting spaces for both public and private conversations.

Our clients are diverse but share one thing in common—the desire for their agency to produce the highest level of creative work possible. We accept no client with less than $1 million in billings. We specialize in challenger brands, working with clients who are willing to take risks in order to gain momentum against the leader in their category. Our relationships with our clients, and what they have to say about us, is what drives our growth and attracts new business.

We offer the highest level of service and creativity in a variety of disciplines, with a focus in advertising, public relations, social marketing, interactive, and design. We are producing the kind of creative work across all disciplines that wins awards, but that is not our motivation. We are masters of new technology and use it for all our creative executions. We use the word *media* in its broadest context. We are well known as leaders in marketing due to our creative application of ideas to non-traditional situations.

Our clients describe us as their marketing partner—the word *vendor* is never mentioned in relation to our firm. We are regularly sought as industry experts by media and forums seeking expert opinions and speakers on innovative marketing. We are inundated with the resumes of amazing and talented people who want to be part of our team.

Our team members are highly trained, excellent communicators who are clear about their goals and vision. Every person has been chosen for a specific purpose and with a common thread—we all demand the highest level of quality and creativity. We are honest, forthright, and possess a high level of integrity and confidence. There are no egomaniacs. Rather, we are a group of well-trained, fun-loving, creative minds with a desire to do fantastic work and be rewarded for it. Our teams are compensated well for their hard work, and they share in the success of the company through profit sharing and bonus programs.

Our leadership style is inspirational and exemplifies the high standards we have set for creativity and success. We are not a punitive atmosphere and are supportive of people learning from their mistakes. We are willing to take risks and allow team members the freedom to take their own.

In this way, the partners created clarity for themselves and produced goals they could share with their growing team. The visualization exercise was also a helpful tool that they could use to inform their decisions going forward. A little more than five years later, they were in their new office. It was a colorful, open space, and they had hired about thirty-five bright, hard-working employees, many of whom were Gen Y. The partners had achieved everything that they had visualized and written down. From that moment of clarity, they were able to build a plan and work toward delivering it.

CLARITY IS A TOOL

So far, all of the leaders we interviewed and shared in this book have had the ability to forge clarity and use it to make a difference. Even when these companies have achieved success in their vision, the leaders continued to communicate and interact with employees because the job is never really done. They must continually provide clarity as priorities shift, new products are launched, new services are created, and new expectations are revealed. All of this works together to make the vision compelling, engaging, and exciting for everyone. It's another approach to engage employees in a way that makes them want to take the stairs two steps at a time on the way to work.

On the other hand, a lack of clarity is a killer. In 2015, INSEAD business school published an article titled "Who Killed Nokia? Nokia Did" (Huy 2016). This article was based on seventy-six interviews with top and middle managers, engineers, and external experts to ascertain where Nokia went wrong. Let's review.

In 2007 Nokia was earning 55 percent of all profits in the mobile phone sector. It was without doubt a hugely successful company, and it dominated the market. And then, almost overnight, Nokia became irrelevant. INSEAD concluded that "organizational fear was grounded in a culture of temperamental leaders and frightened middle managers, scared of telling the truth" (Huy 2016). After the iPhone was launched and began successfully disrupting the market, Nokia's management didn't lead with vision; they chose to continue as before. Managers at different levels received different messages about how to compete against this new threat, confusion swept through the organization, and eventually the culture deteriorated to a point where "fearing the reactions of top managers, middle managers remained silent or provided optimistic, i.e. filtered information. In reality the lack of leadership in the face of adversity had led to key people lying about progress, sales, and ambition" (Huy 2016).

Rather than creating clarity and a realistic way forward, leaders at Nokia were overpromising and underdelivering. In a *Wall Street Journal* article, Alastair Curtis, Nokia's chief designer from 2006 to 2009, described the situation as follows: "You were spending more time fighting politics than doing design" (Troianovski and Grundberg 2012). The organizational structure was so convoluted, he added, that "it was hard for the team to drive through a coherent, consistent, beautiful experience."

James Surowiecki, author of *The Wisdom of Crowds* (2005), wrote a piece in the *New Yorker* that alluded to the lack of visionary leadership:

"Nokia's failure resulted at least in part from an institutional reluctance to transition into a new era" (Surowiecki 2013). This was summed up in a *Harvard Business Review* paper that attributed Nokia's problem to a lack of clarity: "Much of the problem stems from habits of communication that favor unfocused discussions about strategy over clear plans to bring new phone models to market" (Groysberg and Slind 2012).

Nokia, it seems, lurched from one direction to another without getting buy-in from employees or giving them the clarity required to do their jobs effectively. In 2013 Nokia was bought by Microsoft for a fraction of what its capitalization had been in 2007. INSEAD summarized the key issues: "Nokia's top managers should have encouraged and role-modeled more authentic and psychologically safe dialogue, internal coordination and feedback mechanisms to understand the true emotional picture in the organization. They might then have been able to better gauge what was possible and what was not, and most importantly, what to do about it" (Huy 2016).

Today Nokia is in a much better position, but during that time Nokia didn't have a clear vision. Their people were disengaged with the company, and the lack of clarity led to a culture of deceit and self-interest. This is in complete contrast to what we have learned so far: visionary leaders actively encourage selfless behavior at every level and, where possible, create communities built on trust and respect. As we saw, Chris Lofaso created clarity at all three levels of his organization, which resulted in the best financial results for ten years and a party at Bodega Bay. Clarity is a tool, and smart leaders must learn how to use it effectively.

THE CLARITY OF CONVERSATION

In a world where virtual is hip and convenient, there is still something to be said for getting face-to-face and having a conversation to establish greater clarity. This was a lesson that one of the CEOs we spoke with learned as a leader.

Robert was CEO of a well-known global consumer brand who managed Northern Europe. Every year, Robert's company flew their top eighty managers to Stockholm for the annual two-day management conference. The agenda and setup were just like a thousand other conferences: market updates, product innovations, consumer trends, investment strategies, and the chance to network with colleagues over dinner.

In 2015 the business was going through some cost-cutting efforts, and the leaders believed that it would send the wrong message to fly eighty managers to a respectable hotel for two days while it was asking employees to find ways to save money. Instead, Robert and his CFO, Andreas, traveled to each of the four countries that he managed and organized a strategy session with the local management team.

In each country, they met with the top fifteen managers to discuss the same topics they would have discussed during their conference. They created an agenda that was structured but interactive, and it resulted in a candid exchange of ideas and allowed for questions from those closest to the work. The questions challenged what was being presented and raised important issues. The day became a conversation instead of a series of presentations. Robert began to realize that he would never have received such a significant level of feedback if he had presented from an elevated stage to a room of eighty people; these face-to-face meetings provided clarity, not just for his managers but for him also. He recognized that they would be a stronger organization as a result.

After the "strategy tour," the company asked the managers to evaluate satisfaction and outcome. The feedback was overwhelming, especially in contrast to the feedback for the traditional annual meeting. Here are some of the common responses.

"Finally, the CEO and CFO are really listening to us."

"I liked having a real conversation—it was a productive give and take."

"I really felt like I was able to contribute."

"Now I understand where we're going—and how I can contribute to our goals."

Robert and Andreas invested more of their own time than in previous years, but they gained in return a much deeper level of insight about the markets, and they created a stronger bond with the management team. Robert's managers felt energized and informed, they were clear about what was expected of them, and they were eager to implement the strategies that had been discussed. They also felt they could provide clarity to their own teams.

Even though Generation Y employees are the first digital natives and digital communication is exciting, convenient, and often fun, it isn't always best. Forging clarity also means taking the time to determine the best way to communicate as well as the best content. Our next challenge was to gain a deeper understanding of connectedness, which is what we will cover in our next chapter.

TAKEAWAYS FROM CHAPTER 6

- Clarity is the thread that extends from the vision to individual personal objectives.
  - Test your vision on some trusted individuals who are not connected with your work; if they understand it then your employees will.
- There are three levels of clarity: organizational, workgroup, and individual.
  - It is worth reviewing and auditing your internal processes for two-way communication, governance at each level, and appraisal and personal development plans to ensure that your vision will be embedded.
  - Consider how you will cascade your messages and measure success.
- Clarity defines accountability and responsibility; it sets expectations that allow people to work efficiently and effectively.
  - If you are taking your organization forward in a new direction, you will want to review your organizational structure and the roles and responsibilities throughout the organization.

- As a leader you will also have your own personal objectives to aim for and recognize areas where you may need further support or personal development in order to lead effectively—what are the three areas that you most need to develop in the next twelve months?

- Write your own narrative of what you will be doing in five years from now: describe the organization you work for, the type of work you do, your customers, and the people you work with. What does success look like for you?

CHAPTER 7

Build Connectivity

Connecting with generation y presents a looming challenge for leaders, but that challenge can also be turned into a great opportunity. As we met with leaders, reviewed the organizational connectedness (OC) research, and reviewed our experiences, we searched for the attributes of an organization that nurtured connectivity. We asked ourselves if we had ever felt deeply connected to an organization.

Connecting with Generation Y presents a looming challenge for leaders, but that challenge can also be turned into a great opportunity.

John and I agreed that we had both felt and still feel deeply connected to CPP, Inc., where we were both employed when we met. CPP is publisher of the Myers-Briggs Type Indicator® (MBTI®) and other well-known assessments. For us, the attribute that connected us was a feeling of pride to be a part of something that we believed was meaningful. Their vision is to be the world leader in personality, career, and organizational development assessments, and we felt that they actually were the world leader in the quality, power, and reputation of the assessments. MBTI® was, and still is, one of the most widely used personal diagnostic assessment tools to help people understand themselves and each other. CPP was birthed out of that same impulse to understand and help—and it still carried that mission forward. We were really proud to be a part of the CPP story. We were proud to tell the story to customers, and we were proud to work with and teach others to work with such high-quality tools. There were times when we would teach an MBTI® program and participants would cry, because they were so happy or relieved to learn about their own and others' personalities. The work was meaningful. It touched people's lives, and since we taught other educators and practitioners how to use the assessments, we felt like our impact was twofold: once for the practitioners and again for all of those people they would work with in the future.

As we discussed in chapter 4, building organizational connectivity means using a vision to create an emotional connection for employees. Even more specifically, it means building an emotional connection for each employee as an individual. It is the ability to bring a concept, your vision, to life and for each employee to understand the impact of their behaviors and actions. We can measure it through loyalty and the willingness of employees to extend effort to help the organization reach its vision and execute on its strategy. When you build connectivity, people don't just take the stairs two steps at time to get to the office; they are willing to go the extra mile in their work, and they do that because they believe in the work they are doing and feel connected to the organization they work for. What's more, they are proud to say who they work for. It's a badge of honor.

Connectedness is the glue that ties the intangible and invisible vision to the tangible and visible employees and their actions.

Since Gen Y will make up 75 percent of the workforce by 2025, it's more important than ever to understand what, if anything, connects them to an organization. With this generational shift, the workforce is changing, and expectations are shifting in ways that will require even greater efforts to create connectedness. As with Coresystems, Uber, and Airbnb, more and more people are able to make a living without having to become employees. Attracting and retaining great talent, whether employed or contracted, will be even trickier for organizations in the future.

As we prepared material for this chapter, Simon told us about a company that has learned how to do connectedness really well. OluKai is a young and hip ocean lifestyle company located in Orange County, California. In fact, they've achieved organizational connectivity in spite of being owned by private equity, a combination that we really didn't expect to find.

THE OLUKAI STORY

OluKai was founded in 2006 by three industry veterans and an investor who realized that there were no high-quality, premium-value sandals on the market, only regular footwear and flip-flops. This was a rare opportunity, a new product category, which in this case was high-priced, premium-quality, comfortable sandals. As with all new product categories, it was clearly risky. After all, if the world was eagerly waiting for high-priced sandals to arrive, then why hadn't they been delivered before? Still, OluKai took the risk and began to build a future with a few critical success ingredients.

Simon interviewed OluKai's CEO, Jim Harris, at their new office building in Irvine, California. We wanted to learn more about the vision of the organization and the philosophy underlying the company strategy. Through Simon's interview with Jim, we saw connectedness in action as Jim peeled back the layers that made this organization a place where employees feel that they are a part of the story.

Jim has been involved with the company since 2008; he took over as CEO in 2011. Prior to working at OluKai Jim had a strong track record of working for luxury brands. "I believe down deep inside of people, each of us," he said, "there is a happy place. It's a place of love, for lack of a better term. We call it *Aloha*. It is a Hawaiian word and means a lot of things.

It means *life, love, hello,* and it also means *goodbye.* It's a very complex word. The literal meaning of *Aloha* is 'the breath of life.' It comes from *Alo,* meaning *presence,* and *ha,* meaning *breath. Aloha* is a way of living and treating each other with love and respect.

"At OluKai, we want to connect with people in a way that brings out that emotion and allows them to live with affection and delight. Our vision is grounded in our belief that everybody, no matter where you are, you can live *Aloha,* a life full of love and happiness. Our brand is one way to unlock that spirit in all of us. We want people who wear a pair of OluKai sandals to connect emotionally to a place and a lifestyle to which they aspire. Maybe they may have never been to a beautiful beach in Hawaii, but they know they want to go. Our footwear brings people one step closer. It's a highly aspirational message that we are delivering."

"At OluKai, we want to connect with people in a way that brings out that emotion and allows them to live with affection and delight."

—Jim Harris

Jim described the company's personal purpose to live *Aloha.* "That is what we are trying to help people do every day. Good things happen in Hawaii. It's a great place. Walking on the beach, hikes up the river, waterfall swims, great food, active lifestyle, and amazing sunsets. It's always wonderful. So, we help people bring a little of that back into their everyday lives, no matter where they are. In doing so we connect with our customers, our employees, and our community."

Jim also shared the ways that the company connects with its customers. "We try to connect with people on an emotional level in a number of different ways. Our products are really only one of the ways we connect, and they are no more important than any other means. We also connect through our 'walk stories,' which can be viewed on our website *(www.olukai.com/walk-stories.html),* through social media channels, and through our points of sale. We connect with people through our retail partnerships, our consumer branding, and our nonprofit organization, Ama OluKai Foundation. We connect with people through our events and sponsorships. Everything we do is intended to create a real emotional connection. We want everyone associated with our brand to feel *Aloha*, and we put a lot of effort into this."

Early in his career, Jim Harris learned a lot about emotional connectedness in the wine and food industry, where people often connect with something other than their mind. He'd noticed how people connect with these kinds of brands through their stomachs and their hearts. He'd seen people become emotionally connected to a winery, because that's where they fell in love, where they became engaged, or where they visited on their honeymoon. He saw that their loyalty was less about the wine and more about their experiential connection. OluKai is very similar. OluKai represent a connection to the islands, to Hawaii, to *Aloha*. When people wear OluKai products, they think about their dream to go there or their time in Hawaii on a vacation, surf trip, or honeymoon. Whatever the reason, OluKai is often a part of that: a very warm emotional connection between the customers and the brand.

ENSURING CONNECTEDNESS TO THE BRAND

OluKai believes that everybody, no matter where they are, can live *Aloha*. Jim became involved with OluKai shortly after it started, working first as its lead board member and then as CEO. In the CEO role, he focused on both the connection and the hope of the brand. He also concentrated on the more tactical business side of running the organization, such as product strategy and overseeing all aspects of the business's success, including the balance sheet, working capital, growth, and distribution strategy.

Jim further explained the approach he took to build the brand. He said, "Building the brand was an evolutionary process. We challenged ourselves with many questions:

- How are we going to execute a premium footwear brand?
- How are we going to make really great, comfortable footwear consistently and do it with a design signature that is recognized as of an island lifestyle?
- How do we create an emotional connection to generate our disproportionate share of mind and wallet? What are the touch points?
- How do we present ourselves in stores, online, and in social media?"

It took them time to answer these searching questions, but the result is that they have been very thoughtful in how they implement their brand strategy. Jim continued, "Purposefully we selected a different price point from brands in our category, such as Reef, Billabong, Quicksilver, or Roxy. Our price points pick up where our competitors' price points drop off. That sets us apart in the industry, and that is why we don't have many direct competitors. Our sandals range from $65 all the way up to one hundred twenty or one hundred thirty dollars for a pair. They are premium quality leather. There's a comfort story. We thought about how much people pay for a pair of jeans or other clothing and asked ourselves, 'Why wouldn't people invest in their feet?' Your feet support your whole body, and you know how it is when you don't wear comfortable shoes? It can ruin your day."

Jim said that some orthopedic doctors are even recommending OluKai products to their patients. The company has received unsolicited testimonials even though they've never reached out to any doctors or tried to sell to the medical industry. That's just an organic result of the quality of their products.

The brand's philosophy connects with what their customers value most. And that's expressed on their website *(www.olukai.com)*, too: "We produce products we believe in. Products we can stand behind. We believe in quality of product and material, craftsmanship in construction and finding quality in life by the choices we make every day." It's this focus on connectedness that is growing the brand.[1]

---

[1] *https://www.OluKai.com/about.html* a watch 2-min video to get a feel for the brand.

OluKai has done well and will continue to grow smartly. They are very strategic about their growth and their distribution plan. They have worked hard to connect with everyone who touches their brand, so they don't want to mess up that connection by being careless. OluKai is very selective in who they partner with because they want to ensure the premium brand experience will come through at the retail level. This, for example, caused them to stay away from big-box stores like Costco. Jim explained, "We have to get the distribution plan right, because it's about the experience and it's about the quality. It's not about the quantity. So far, we've been very successful doing that, and our representatives are able to take our philosophy with them on the road. It's a very, very, high-end selective process that we established and are diligently following that is growing new customers and employees."

PROMOTING THE SPIRIT OF *OHANA*

With OluKai, connectedness extends to everything, particularly the brand's relationship with its employees. Everyone who works at or with OluKai comes together as a true family. They call it *Ohana*, which is Hawaiian for *family*.

> *Everyone who works at or with OluKai comes together as a true family.*

When they have sales meetings, they don't call them sales meetings. Instead, they call them *Makahiki*, which is a Hawaiian word for *reunion* or *gathering*. They even try not to have a corporate sales focus in these gatherings. Rather, it is an opportunity twice a year to come together with their employees and salespeople and celebrate real kinship. They come together to discuss the business they want to create, and they focus on the right partners, the right products, and how to build their business the right way, sustainably and ethically. They work to keep a real eye toward having a company that in twenty years will be the most important ocean lifestyle brand in the United States. It's not a meeting intended to drive performance for the next three to six months. Their focus is on the long road, the future, and it's completely transparent. They do like to reward the team, but they do that with ad hoc recognition as well as economic and emotional recognition for achievements toward the long term.

Clearly, Jim doesn't approach his role in the same way as many CEOs. Whereas some CEOs and their organizations are constantly sprinting from one objective to another, which results in burnout and lack of direction, Jim leads OluKai like they are on a long walk, kicking the sand as they go, making friends along the way. The result is that the further they get, the bigger the crowd that is following.

OluKai is structured within thirteen regions around the United States. Each region has managing representatives and junior and associate salespeople. In similar businesses, the incentives in sales programs are all geared toward the managing salesperson, toward the leader of that territory (although most of the work is done by the associate sales representatives). At OluKai they deliberately focus incentives and rewards on associate sales representatives to ensure that the people who are on the street, getting the accounts, are the ones being recognized for their work.

Another important aspect of OluKai's connection with its employees is the use of imagery. Jim explains, "We do it every meeting to just continue to reinforce what OluKai is. The first thing that we ask our salespeople is to talk about living *Aloha*. We want to intentionally help them transfer to the state of mind of our consumers and their emotional connectedness to our brand."

An important aspect of OluKai's connection with its employees is the use of imagery.

A sense of history is also important to Jim. He says, "We hold our sales meeting in coastal environments, representing the ocean lifestyle. They are more like a reunion or a celebration of our relationship with our team.

We ensure that meals are done in a way that feels like a family reception rather than a corporate event. We have photography around the meeting, showing the history of the company in a way that is like what a family photo album might look like. We always want to remember our history while defining our future."

Aloha and the family concept are embedded throughout the organizational culture. Twice each week employees are offered a complimentary lunch. At the corporate office, they usually have about sixty people gathering and enjoying lunch together, connecting with each other. This happens across all the other offices as well, no matter how big or small the team is there. Birthdays, anniversaries, new babies, weddings, and engagements are all celebrated.

"We feel it's important that we connect in a personal way," Jim explained. And that's clear.

Jim and his team also organize team-building events four times a year. They shut the office for the entire day and go out as a team in order to bond and foster team spirit. They might go to the beach, go surfing, do stand-up paddling, rent boats and have internal competition racing, go to baseball games—you name it. Every year they do something different, but it always reflects the spirit of the brand.

Cheryl, the director for Human Resources, said that the connection to OluKai is deep. Cheryl is quick on her feet, witty, decisive, and dynamic in her thinking, but for years she struggled to find a company that was the right fit for her. Either she would get bored, or the culture was dysfunctional, or the company was stagnant. Each time she would move on and try a new opportunity, but eventually she found OluKai, where she has been for more than ten years. She's stayed because at OluKai she feels connected.

As Cheryl noted, the people at OluKai are like a family. They truly and genuinely care about the brand, so leaders are able to unleash an entrepreneurial spirit where employees will do whatever it takes for the good of the brand. It's not just the job description that they're working toward; they have a personal interest in the company. They understand that when they give, they get. According to Cheryl, "Employees really feel a personal ownership in the company and a sense of pride." She said, "It shows in the performance and attitude of our people. They are willing to give of themselves. They are going above and beyond all the time, and that's definitely part of the success of their brand."

We can see from what Jim and Cheryl have said that OluKai creates connectedness by sharing and communicating the values and vision for the brand regularly. Employees like to have fun every day. They build relationships based on trust and respectful communications. They perform with honesty and integrity. They work together and help each other be accountable. They take risks and are encouraged to learn from their mistakes. They balance life and work. They find unexpected solutions. They work together to lessen their impact on the environment. They find a way to make a difference and do great things. They believe in themselves and in their *Ohana*. That's the OluKai way.

And the result? There is a very low turnover of staff at OluKai. Many employees who started with the company are still there today. This is really important to Jim, because to recruit, place, and train new talent is very costly and difficult for a company with such a strong culture. Initially, it sounds like the work is leisurely—the pace reflects a stroll along the beach and not much work gets done—but in reality, the opposite is true. Productivity is very high at OluKai, because employees appreciate what is provided for them. It's not unusual to see people at their desks, working and having fun, at seven or eight o'clock in the evening. As Cheryl succinctly put it, "I'm just eager to take care of business. It's a passion."

Cheryl's sense of connection with the company was palpable and genuine. She said that she honestly enjoyed working with everyone there. She also believed that she was learning from Jim all the time. She felt that she could make mistakes and have an opportunity to learn from them instead of getting in trouble. They are constantly pushing forward. That is why she is still there after ten years!

COMBINING PRIVATE EQUITY VALUES WITH FAMILY VALUES

Before OluKai, Jim spent half of his career in private equity, mainly investing in leading premium consumer product companies. He learned as much as he could about value creation in different companies. But he was never really comfortable with the transactional nature of private equity. Typically, in private equity, there is a desire to leverage the balance sheet and bleed profits out of margin enhancements—often short-term gains at long-term costs. There is a lot of cash management focus, which is part of the script.

But Jim wanted to dig deeper with the teams and be more present in the creation of value after the acquisition was done. He wanted to create value in a broader sense, not only equity value: value to the trade, value to consumers, and value to the various stakeholders.

He explained, "I wanted to engage more holistically with a company and see the impact, not only on employees but also on their families. In my office at OluKai, I have pictures of my family on my walls, but I've also got pictures of our employees and their families too. I think companies need to recognize that they are ultimately providing for a lot more than just an employee's well-being. They're providing for their families' well-being too. I think companies forget that they participate in the broader community."

This is the same sentiment employed by Todd Bastean at BNA. For him it was a recognition that employees have families, and he has a responsibility to make sure that each employee goes home safely at the end of each day. Todd, like Jim, looked beyond the people in the room and thought about where they came from each morning and where they went back to at the end of the day.

Jim explained, "A lot of what has impacted my attitude and business mind-set is rooted in a very basic concept my father constantly reiterated: treat other people with respect. That's how we built the organization, and it's how we build our retail partnership. Everything we have done, we've done as if we were doing it for our own family and friends or for ourselves. We honor our word. We care about emotions. We care about people. We care about the long term. I think about managing businesses as if you are a parent. I have four kids. This company is like my fifth child. We focus on developing and nurturing this business as if we are nurturing a child."

Importantly, this emphasis on connectedness has not been at the expense of growth and profit. Jim continued, "At OluKai without having excessive leverage on the balance sheet, we have been able to grow over the years by using our income statement and reinvesting our profits. We've been able to invest ahead of the curve in building the right organization for our company. And that has proven to be very lucrative in terms of revenue growth and profit. We have seen a return of more than 30 percent on investment from activities related to trade spending and to organizational development. This would have been impossible in a leveraged environment."

CREATING AN OFFICE THAT FEELS LIKE HOME

One thing we noticed as we reviewed this interview is that everything about OluKai is a story, and that these stories serve as the foundation of the philosophies that connect the employees.

For example, when they moved into a new office in 2016, they tried to tie the building and aesthetics to their heritage, their roots in Hawaii. The accent paint colors on the walls were inspired by the land and the ocean. The blue represents the ocean, and the red represents the red sands, the mud, and the earth in Maui. There are wooden desks and wooden tables, primarily made from koa wood, which is a very valued wood from Hawaii. It's regarded as very sacred, and it gives the office a tropical feel. The countertops in the lobby of the building are basalt, which is a lava rock. This creates a connection to the islands and their volcanic origins.

They use a lot of natural materials throughout the space. The ropes that are used throughout the building to hold up the hanging shelves are representative of something the natives would use to construct boats and houses in Hawaii. By the reception desk in the lobby, the whole wall is made out of stone. It is reminiscent of the shell of the sea turtle, and it's really interesting how the light reflects off of it just as the sun would reflect off the turtle's shell in the ocean.

Even the drywall, which is behind the front reception desk, is reminiscent of waves. It's very subtle, but there are waves across the whole wall. Around the outside of the building, there are footprints in the concrete—the footprints of OluKai footwear. It's cool. There are also murals painted on the walls to depict the legend of Naupaka by the sea. Naupaka is a rare type of plant that can be found only on the Big Island, where it is extremely common.

All of this works well to make the environment more like a home instead of a sterile, corporate set of offices. The environment reflects the whole spirit and life of the company.

Cheryl confirmed these findings for us. "We all love it here," she said. "It feels like home."

A CULTURE OF CONNECTEDNESS

As these sections have shown, the OluKai story is rich in connectedness. They have a culture that is built around a continuous focus on connecting—from the brand, to the building, to the employees, to their customers. Even beyond that, they stay focused on connecting to their history, their community, and their environment. They are focused on connecting from the top of the organization to the bottom.

In many organizations there is greater connectedness on the front line, but it weakens as people travel up through the corporate hierarchy. For instance, in many cases, employees on the front lines are working in the trenches together. They are barbecuing and going to ball games, carpooling, and working out babysitters together. They are living and working and caring for each other. But then as people start to climb the ladder, they begin to lose that closeness, that connectedness. Competition increases, often causing the bonds that kept employees close to loosen. In our work, John, Simon, and I have noticed that leaders often show less interpersonal connectedness as they rise higher and higher. In fact, many have been encouraged to separate themselves by well-meaning managers or mentors.

The emerging workforce demands authenticity.

However, behavior isn't inborn and unchangeable. It can—and possibly should—evolve over time. Our interpersonal need for connectedness doesn't change as we rise through the organization, so behaving as if it has lessened can be disingenuous. The emerging workforce won't stand for it. They demand authenticity, so reviewing success stories like OluKai is a good way for us to learn how it can be done at every level. While every culture is different and will approach connectedness differently, we can learn the concepts that work from those who have already walked the path. What makes the OluKai environment particularly interesting is that they are intentionally connecting in a personal way throughout the entire organization and beyond.

THE PROCESS FOR CREATING
A COMPELLING VISION

An underlying component of creating a compelling vision that engages others is the intentional aspect of process. The process for creating the vision matters at least as much as—and maybe even more than at times—the vision itself.

- A relatively simple vision can be set alight by an engaging process: one that excites, inspires, provides context, and connects boldly with emotions and aspirations. This kind of process allows space for:
  - Others to contribute.
  - The vision to become relevant.
  - Delivering clear examples.
  - Guiding the way people think, work, and behave.

And when we say *set alight*, that is exactly what we mean. A vision should positively shine with interest, excitement, and passion. Employees will be taking the stairs two steps at a time on the way to work and investors will be looking to buy the stock. Suppliers will be showcasing their work for your business, and your customers' visits to your website will be growing quickly.

Unfortunately, not all leaders follow an engagement process or give it the focus required to achieve a truly compelling vision. This results in a vision that is flat, dull, and uninspiring, which ultimately culminates in a lack of connectedness. We sometimes see chief strategy or chief experience officers (CXOs) who are fixated on creating an exciting, ingenious, and "perfect" vision. But sometimes, by fixating on "ingenious perfection," they apply a process that is weak, flawed, or nonexistent, and the vision struggles to gain any traction and influence at all.

The process for creating the vision and putting it to work matters as much as the vision. So, what is that process?

1. *Imagine a dream.* Consider what could be achieved, what success would look like, and what it would mean for you personally as well as for your team, business, and future.

2. *Check the dream.* Discuss it, get buy-in, and solicit reflections from other leaders. Focus on how it could be improved and enhanced, and who would benefit and when.

3. *Create multiple options and routes to achieving the dream.* Use a process of fast prototyping that allows for deviation from the map and leaves people feeling empowered and with the ability (permission and opportunity) to get involved. Allow for risk, innovation, and the potential for setbacks.

4. *Communicate it in a way that connects emotionally with anyone whose energies and attention are needed.* Steer the process of messaging and storytelling. Taking the right approach is vital because it cascades the message down through the organization and beyond: connecting with employees and customers, shaping the culture and brand, and guiding the decisions that are taken and the way people work.

5. *Personalize the vision.* Be sure to help people understand their role in achieving the vision. For example, let them know what they need to do more of or better, what they need to stop doing, and where they need to start. Appeal to their own self-interests. For example, if they like stimulating, original work, show them how

that plays a part. If they are concerned about new challenges and progression, show them where they can have an impact. Visions need to be simple, but they also need to be rich, adaptable, and able to fit in any context.

There are, of course, exceptions to the process rule, most notably when employees and stakeholders already buy in to the vision and drive of a powerful, charismatic leader. Consider Jack Ma, Richard Branson, Indra Nooyi, Arianna Huffington, Elon Musk, Jeff Bezos, or Steve Jobs. They built their companies around their own established visions. But even these leaders' visions yield results that can be measured while connecting powerfully with people. They offer clarity, they show courage, and, as a result, they create cultures where the vision is actively put to work. In any case, just because there are a few exceptions doesn't mean that organizations should take a pass on process. Most organizations will be much more successful at creating a compelling vision if the process for getting there is carefully thought out and developed.

In every instance we examined, we discovered that engaging employees around a compelling vision is tied closely to the culture of the organization. That is what we will tackle next.

TAKEAWAYS FROM CHAPTER 7

- What are the positive messages that you can use to help people connect with your vision?
- Don't hold a meeting; have a *Makahiki*.
- Create stories that people can buy in to and share.
- Be aware that the higher you rise in an organization, the less connected you may become, and that you will need to work harder to stay connected and know how to engage your employees.
- Describe your current culture and check if it fits with the culture that you think is required to deliver your vision. What do you need to reshape?

- The process of creating a vision and engaging people around it is often just as important as the vision itself. Create an engagement plan and give it the focus it deserves.

CHAPTER 8

Shape Culture

"CULTURE EATS EVERYTHING for Breakfast, Lunch and Dinner" (Bina 2016). This was the title of a recent *Insigniam Quarterly*'s Letter from the Editor. Most of us know Peter Drucker's famous quote "Culture eats strategy for breakfast," but John, Simon, and I liked this quote even better. It reminds us just how all-consuming culture can be.

> *"Culture Eats Everything for Breakfast, Lunch and Dinner."*

Culture is the pattern of behavior and mind-set that is encouraged or discouraged by people and processes over time. It doesn't matter what you *say* your culture is; how the majority behaves is what determines what the culture *really* is. If you say that you have a culture that empowers people but you have systems, processes, and managers that don't allow people to make decisions, then your real culture could be described as not trusting your employees, which is the complete opposite of empowerment. Creating the right culture—and maintaining it over time—is an essential skill for visionary leaders.

As we started to think about the topic of culture, we knew it was a hot issue among leadership and management educators. We also knew that culture is a very important part of leading with vision, so again we wanted to find organizations that lead with vision and do culture well. The companies we showcase in this chapter do an exemplary job of creating a culture that inspires employees to achieve the vision.

CULTURE AT THE CENTER OF A GLOBAL COMPANY: HILTI CORPORATION

One company with an inspiring culture is the Hilti Corporation, a global construction equipment manufacturer. To find out more, we arranged an interview with Eivind Slaaen, head of People and Culture Development at Hilti.

Eivind, a Norwegian, has been with Hilti in Switzerland for a total of twenty-five years and has spent the last nine years as head of People and Culture Development. Fortunately, Simon was also able to arrange to meet the current chairman of the board, Professor Dr. Pius Baschera, who served as Hilti's CEO from 1994 to 2006. Our goal for the meetings was to discover how Hilti had successfully leveraged culture as a competitive advantage and a tool to achieve their vision and execute their strategy.

> *Culture can be a competitive advantage. It's a tool that can be used to achieve the vision and executive on the strategy.*

By way of background, Hilti (Hilti Aktiengesellschaft or Hilti AG, also known as Hilti Group) was founded in 1941 by Martin and Eugen Hilti. Martin was a mechanical engineer. He started with the company working in the mechanical workshop—producing equipment and components on contract for German industry during World War II (Company History 2016).

Today, the company supplies leading-edge technology to construction professionals worldwide. Their products, systems, and services offer innovative solutions to customers in the construction, building maintenance, and mining industries ("Home—Hilti Corporation" n.d). Many of their customers have a need for specialized drills and fasteners (Hindle 2011).

Hilti's impressively large and beautiful headquarters sit at the base of a mountain in the town where Martin and Eugen founded the company—Schaan—in the principality of Liechtenstein. Schaan has a population of 5,900 people, while Hilti employs more than 23,000 people in over 120 countries. Hilti's 2015 revenues were 4.4 billion Swiss francs, and they are privately owned by the Martin Hilti Family Trust. This has placed Michael Hilti and his family at number 228 on the *Forbes* list of the World's Richest People.

FRONT AND CENTER: CULTURE AND INNOVATION

Hilti is known for culture and innovation. They've won numerous awards for this, including being named AON Hewitt Best Employer, Europe's Great Places to Work, Fortune 100 Best Companies to Work For, and the Sunday Times 100 Best Companies to Work For. They've also won awards for innovation, including the Good Design Award, the Product Design Award, and the Red Dot Award. The company invests as much as 5.5 percent of their revenue annually toward research and development, producing over forty new products every year.

Their vision is to "passionately create enthusiastic customers and build a better future," and their mission statement sets out the aims of the company's culture:

> To create enthusiastic customers, we create success for our customers by identifying their needs and providing differentiated and value-adding solutions.
>
> To build a better future, we:
>
> - Foster a company climate in which every team member is valued and able to grow.
> - Develop win-win relationships with our partners and suppliers.

- Embrace our responsibility toward society and the environment.
- Aim to achieve sustainable value creation, thus securing our freedom of action. ("Vision and Values—Hilti Corporation" n.d.)

NUTS AND BOLTS: THE PROCESS
OF DEVELOPING A CULTURE

The interview with Eivind Slaaen was designed to understand the depth of the culture. The interview with Pius Baschera was designed to understand the strategic mind-set of the leadership team.

According to Eivind, Hilti has always been a company of evolution—not revolution—having been in business for seventy-five years. For decades now, they have applied a structured strategy development process, taking time every five years or so to step back and look at what has changed. They evaluate current trends and review strategy in light of those trends. They aim to determine what is working, what is not working, and whether or not their team is in the right place to take the company into the future.

From 1996 to 2013, Hilti had a strategy called *Champion 3C— Customer, Competence, Concentration*. During that same time period, they also had two rounds of revisions to the strategy. However, in the aftermath of the financial crisis in 2011, they decided to conduct a deeper analysis and began a full-blown strategy development process.

Hilti brought together their own people from all over the world. They identified geographic regions and markets—United States, Germany, India, China—and diverse business units, plus energy and industry divisions. They wanted to look at trends in each industry, understand what their competitors were doing, and analyze their competitive strategies. They reviewed everything from how they were conducting business to what they needed for future success. It took fifteen months to develop a corporate umbrella strategy, which they named *Champion 2020*. In November 2013 they presented that strategy at a conference to the top 150 managers and leaders within the company.

The core of the strategy was the idea of *Sustainable Value Creation through Leadership and Differentiation*. Their goal is not just to win in the marketplace today, but also to create value for the company over the long term. In order to do this, they strive for market leadership. If they are in a specific field, they must be number one, two, or three, because that's where the money is made. One of their core strategies to achieve this high-market position is through innovation and culture.

Using direct sales, operational excellence, and high-performing global teamwork, Hilti takes the market head on. Unlike their competitors who build sales channels and dealer networks to sell through distributors, Hilti decided to go directly to clients to build and retain those relationships. Although this costs more, it permits them to stay close to the customer and get immediate feedback, allowing them to be customer-centric, responsive, and more innovative than their competitors.

With the direct sales team focusing on both listening to and delivering for customers, Hilti has successfully launched more than forty innovations in new products and new business models. They've effectively used operational excellence to get lean and to create efficient processes throughout the company. Finally, they have put their strategies to work by using global teamwork to deliver innovative products and services.

Hilti has a lot of employees, which makes their business model costly. In order to be financially sound, they need products that command a higher margin. The Hilti direct sales force works closely with customers to monitor and advise about the use of Hilti products. That is how the direct sales team discovers their customers' needs, which they are then able to use to inform the innovation process. Without this team competency, they would lack a strategic advantage. Hilti builds everything around engaging their people in this high-performance environment; they've created a culture that is both caring and performance oriented.

TESTING AND IMPLEMENTING A CORPORATE VISION

Hilti goes beyond the norm when it comes to engaging their employees. They want their workforce to own the strategies and to understand the key role each person plays in enhancing the corporate vision and goals.

In 1996 Pius Baschera, who was then serving as CEO, wanted to test whether employees would understand the corporate vision and whether or not they would get behind it. At their headquarters in Schaan, Pius personally led a four-hour workshop with fifteen employees from the assembly line. He used a small group to test whether his training method would be clear to the larger employee base. He set up multiple flip charts and discussed the core pillars of the strategy. He shared with the group how the strategy would have a positive impact on production.

The format was a standing meeting, so everyone was walking around and conversing. After two hours, Pius asked the team leader whether they should take a break. The team leader responded, "Absolutely, but not because we're tired of standing. After all, we stand at the assembly line for eight hours every day. We need a break because our heads are starting to heat up!"

Pius realized he needed to simplify the strategy message. People need to be able to get it immediately, and if after two hours they were still struggling, then something was wrong. Pius also knew that it would be pointless to pursue a strategy that only he fully understood, because it would never be delivered, no matter how good the slides looked. The team needed to go revisit the strategy, break it down, and create a compelling story that employees could connect to and get behind.

> *The team needed to go revisit the strategy, break it down, and create a compelling story that employees could connect to and get behind.*

When they finalized their new strategy, *Champion 2020*, Hilti management concentrated on taking complex strategic topics and explaining them in a clear and approachable way. Four months later, they introduced a half-day workshop, *Experience Champion 2020*, an interactive session designed to take all the elements of the strategy, pull them apart, and make them clear to each employee. They took thirty people at a time through the workshop, with general managers leading the training. Ultimately they ran 775 sessions in six months and reached 22,000 people. The workshops were highly engaging, with a focus on exploring each employee's role, contribution, and goals.

The Hilti strategy workshops built on the idea that the people in the room were the champions. They didn't engage them with PowerPoint presentations, but through dialogue. They also took the training out to the people. The workshops were held in the repair shops, the warehouses, and wherever the sales teams were working. They made the strategy relevant for each person.

Since everyone was expected to complete the training, each person had the same framework: the focus of the company and each individual's role in it. Today, every Hilti employee—whether field sales rep, marketing person, engineer, or production manager—can explain the strategy and how their individual role affects the value creation process.

BUILDING INNOVATION INTO THE CULTURE

Uncovering Customer Need

A major part of the Hilti go-to-market strategy is innovation, a strategy that, Eivind said, is often driven by their close relationship with and understanding of their clients' needs.

Because the Hilti direct sales team spends time with customers, they are sometimes able to uncover needs that the customers didn't even realize they had. For instance, they sometimes use video case studies of projects to establish how they can help customers improve efficiencies with their power tools, particularly steps to reduce productivity losses on-site. One particular video case study showed that their customers were spending a significant portion of their time measuring in advance of drilling a hole, because the measuring process required a ladder and two people.

Hilti employees were able to take that observation and bring a new positioning instrument into the construction industry. Hilti started a joint venture company, and they subsequently built their own business unit just for this purpose. Innovation is at the heart of the Hilti culture, and they were able to share this success story across the organization to reinforce Hilti's openness to new ideas and to encourage creative thinking.

Innovation in Asset Management

Another big innovation occurred when they flipped their mind-set from selling tools to customers to leasing them, which is called fleet management. Customers pay a monthly fee for usage of the equipment but do not own it. Hilti ships the products to the construction sites, repairs them when they break, manages inventory, and upgrades them with newer models.

Hilti ON!Track is another innovative professional solution for customers to manage all their tool and machine assets. Customers can use it to track what assets they have, track where they are assigned, input their condition, and note which employee is responsible. The program also assists in tracking the history of all assets and proactively managing repairs and inspections. Customers appreciate the simplicity. Without the responsibilities of ownership and the need to make big investments in their equipment, they have the right tools at the right location at the right time.

Hilti's intentional culture is to be caring and performance oriented. A lot of other companies say they want a culture like that, but many are unable to achieve it. Hilti's differentiator is that culture is an ongoing focus—not a topic-of-the-day issue.

Founder Martin Hilti, a man with a high degree of ethical responsibility, also had a lot to do with the culture. At one point he decided to bring in management talent from the outside, but he quickly realized it didn't work; they were politically motivated and were more concerned about who will succeed Martin when he dies! That was the only time Hilti ever hired an executive directly from the outside, and it quickly hit home that culture has a huge impact.

ADJUSTING PROCESSES AND ENCOURAGING EMPLOYEE FLEXIBILITY

Another eye opener occurred about thirty years ago during the first global recession in the construction industry. Hilti was struggling, and their difficulties were also internal; they knew they needed to get serious about codifying a common process for improvements. In 1984, they started culture training.

The first phase was called *Inno* (innovation). It had to do with principles and tactics, such as leaving a circle of habits. The premise was that employees who wanted to grow would have to get out of their comfort zone, with the understanding that this system naturally causes some turbulence while learners are gaining proficiency. In this first phase, they shared philosophies about success and failure to set expectations for a period of adjustment.

They also addressed issues of dealing with change through the concept "love it, leave it or change it." which is an attitude to work that Hilti wanted to encourage. They wanted employees to be committed to work and loving what they do. If someone didn't, then Hilti wanted them to change what they didn't like. If they couldn't do that, they would prefer that the employee left rather than working without enthusiasm for the job. This was a commitment to self—not to others. The employees were making themselves a promise.

They started talking about these ideas throughout the global workforce. At first, they focused on the management teams. Then later they expanded to a wider base. Management communicated to everyone that they were instituting a common set of fundamentals in order to set Hilti apart as a company that addresses the marketplace in a unified way.

CULTURE PLANNING PUTS HILTI
AT THE TOP, GLOBALLY

Now Hilti has a new, more structured process, which they call *Our Culture Journey*. They have clearly defined values. When employees join Hilti, they go through a twelve-hour session broken out over two days in which they learn about and discuss the culture. They cover values, vision, and some of the principles of the organization. Every two years, every team goes through a structured process where they discuss a business topic that is relevant to the company. They decide which behaviors need to be adopted or changed in order to be more successful in the future. It's a process of continuous improvement driven by every individual in the company.

This improvement process cascades through the entire workforce. They discuss what's working well, what's not working well, and how the team is performing. The exercise goes right to a personal level, for feedback and exploration of growth opportunities. It's a vital process. Employees step out of the work environment and evaluate everything so they can see what needs to change. Not only does this reinforce the culture, but it also helps everyone to understand the bigger picture, which is vital for innovation.

They also expect change to start at the individual level. Companies don't change. People change. Teams change. The company is made up of people and teams.

Our Culture Journey has the full support of top management at Hilti, and the company is willing to invest about 25,000 individual employee workdays a year to operate it. That's how important it is.

QUANTIFYING INVESTMENT IN CULTURE

Hilti makes a substantial investment in building a culture, and they use the culture to achieve their vision and execute their strategy. This is a significant point. It wouldn't happen if they weren't willing to make the investment, and they wouldn't be willing to make the investment if the senior management team was not close to the process.

This is a company led by people who do not assume that culture is a Human Resources or Training Department issue—which actually happens often in other corporations. Instead, the leadership team at Hilti really understand their role. They have a vision. They can see when their culture needs to shift in order to support and deliver it, so they take responsibility for making it happen and lead from the top.

We asked Eivind if he feels that their culture is a strategic advantage. He said that it is, because while it's easy for competitors to copy new products, it's very hard—maybe impossible—for them to copy a culture. Hilti's strategic advantage is their attention to and development of a caring and high-performing culture that protects them more in the long term than the short term.

It's easy for competitors to copy new products. It's very hard—maybe impossible—for them to copy a culture.

Eivind also shared that Michael Hilti, son of the founder, believes that culture is a core competence at Hilti. The Hilti culture forces alignment starting at the top. Management understands that they receive the benefits of spending so much time, money, and effort on culture. They aren't trying to measure it. They aren't trying to get a return back in money, and they know how much they're spending on it. It's impossible to quantify the output—so they don't even try—but they see results through many, many other indirect measures.

LEADERSHIP DEVELOPMENT AND RETENTION

One of those indirect measures is leadership development and retention. They believe that their focus on an intentional culture of caring and high performance contributes significantly to both. They develop 80 percent of their leaders from within, and they do this on a global level. This is a company committed to developing leadership from the ranks. They don't hire anyone into the executive board (senior leadership positions) from the outside. The risk of doing that is too high. Instead, they bring outside talent in at the senior level so they will still have fresh blood in the company. But those people are then integrated into the culture long before they make it to the top.

They also believe that their high retention rates are at least partially due to their focus on culture. Their retention rate is 86 percent in their direct sales teams. Most sales companies have a retention rate of around 70 percent.

---

*This means fostering an entrepreneurial spirit,
actively taking initiatives for innovation, and being
willing to take risks.*

They also see payback in terms of engagement. They get a commitment from employees to go the extra mile for the customers, and the customers know it. They know that if they call, Hilti employees will take care of them.

Dr. Baschera shared another distinctive thing about Hilti culture: the CEO succession planning process. Hilti doesn't turn over CEOs often. Many companies change their CEO every three to five years. Many times, other companies bring in a new CEO, and the first thing they do is set a new strategy. Hilti doesn't do it that way. Since the founding of Hilti in 1941, they have had only five CEOs, with an average tenure of fifteen years. Every time they have a change of CEO, they go through an organized and orchestrated strategy development process. The outgoing CEO starts the strategy development process, and then the new CEO takes over and completes the work. They do it together. So the history and tradition are carried forward while the new CEO is preparing to own the strategy and take it into the future.

HILTI'S CULTURE PLANNING ADVICE

Hilti is getting a lot of attention due to their success. Since more and more companies are trying to learn from them, here is their advice. Get alignment within your management team on **a set of values** desired in the culture. It is important for the CEO and the senior team to be aligned around those values. Without that unity, nothing will progress. Choose a few values and then make them tangible to the employees.

When Eivind joined Hilti, they had nine values that were hanging on the wall so they could remember them. Then they decided to get radical, so they changed it to four values: courage, commitment, integrity, and teamwork. Then they made it tangible by asking employees to break it down to living principles to show what each value meant in practical terms. They asked employees to describe in their own words how they would live these principles. Going a step further, they asked their employees to coach each other on these principles. Now, their people can actually explain what integrity means in a sales team or what it means in a repair shop. As a result, their values have become real, concrete, and embedded. They aren't just words on a poster.

1. It's important to make sure that the values get put into practice in the business on a day-to-day basis. If there is a violation of the values, regardless of hierarchy, it must be dealt with and not hidden. There needs to be transparency and communication around the violation so that others can see that the leaders are serious about the way the organization will and will not achieve its vision and execute the strategy.

2. Finally, the process of intentionally building culture is one that takes time. It's a long, long journey. Other companies need to be prepared for that.

Hilti's values—courage, commitment, integrity, and teamwork— appear on a compass in their offices as a symbol that reinforces their culture over time. When they do their culture training, they use this symbol, and they have the team stand in front of a big mirror while they hold it. The message from the exercise is for each person to look at themselves and ask what they can do to reinforce culture, not just look to everybody else to do it. It's about owning the message personally and taking responsibility for it.

Hilti also integrates the four values into their people development programs, including the personal development discussions they have with individuals. Values are key to conversations and interviews when they are hiring people, and they award promotions to those who consistently live and model the values through their behavior and attitude.

The chairman of Hilti, Professor Dr. Pius Baschera, is also deeply passionate about culture. When we interviewed Dr. Baschera, he agreed that the culture is their competitive advantage. He said they believe that the growth of the company goes hand in hand with the personal growth of each employee. The DNA of the Hilti culture is a combination of caring for the people and maintaining a strong performance orientation. Their employees are engaged, motivated, team-oriented, and high-performing.

As Dr. Baschera explained, Hilti balances history with innovation. They want to honor their history and culture, but they also want to evolve. This means fostering an entrepreneurial spirit, actively seeking initiatives for innovation, and being willing to take risks. They have to allow for and tolerate mistakes and maintain a culture where failure and learning from failure aren't punished. They know that innovation is not going to happen without some risk.

Consequently, Hilti also encourages risk taking and innovation. Dr. Baschera explained that two times each year, they have groups present innovation projects to the top fifteen executives. One year, one team was working on a new energy supply device for the drill machines. It was a cartridge about the size of a pill. After two years of innovating, piloting the product, and spending about $15 million, the team came back and proposed that the executive team should stop the project. The team had identified that the chances of a market success were slim and that it wasn't worth pursuing. They could either spend another $10 million for further market testing or pull the plug. Dr. Baschera, then CEO, thanked and then congratulated the team for their efforts and honesty. It was not a failure; it was an experience. Instead of asking, "Who made the mistake?" they asked, "What did we learn?" and, "How can we make it better next time?"

THE VALUE OF CULTURE PLANNING

Hilti is a great example of a company that is using culture to advance its position in the marketplace:

1. You have to start with knowing what you want to achieve, and this has to come from the top.

2. There has to be a commitment to intentionally build a strong culture, and senior leaders have to be willing to invest personally to help drive the culture.

3. It helps if there is structure to the culture development process and even some tools, symbols, and exercises like the compass and the mirror to help employees keep it close and real.

4. The work of building the culture has to be systematic and consistent.

5. There needs to be continuity, which can happen through processes such as a people development system, pay structure, performance strategies, and even succession planning.

Hilti's experience, struggles, and current success teach us that culture and vision are inextricably linked and that both require leadership. The wrong culture could easily pull an organization off course from their vision, and the right culture could create competitive advantage and deliver their vision. However, even if companies get everything right—the compelling vision, the courage, the clarity, the connectedness, and the culture—there will still undoubtedly be obstacles to overcome. In every important endeavor there are barriers to success, so we want to look at the next step, which is identifying potential barriers and ways to overcome them.

TAKEAWAYS FROM CHAPTER 8

- Revisit the description of the culture that you want to create from the previous chapter and refine it.

- What are four or five values you will need to embed in order to bring the culture alive?

- Remember that culture is the sum of behaviors, systems, and processes that employees perceive to be "the way things are done"—as a leader you have to tackle the inconsistencies. Are there any systems, processes, or behaviors that are obstacles to shaping the right culture?

- Culture is led from the top, it's not something you can delegate. As a leader you have to take responsibility for creating the culture.

CHAPTER 9

Obstacles to Leading with Vision

COURAGE, CLARITY, CONNECTEDNESS, AND CULTURE are all leader-driven pieces of the puzzle that must be put together in order for a compelling vision to stick. But, inevitably, there are barriers to the success of the vision. There are the typical, expected obstacles, such as a lack of courage, clarity, and connectedness, as well as a lack of energy from the top of the house. And then there are the more difficult challenges, those knotty complex problems are harder to understand and navigate.

After studying the data to determine the barriers that were the most problematic, we narrowed it down to five major obstacles:

1. A lack of unity
2. Preconceived notions
3. A lack of buy-in, filtered down through the organization
4. A lack of urgency
5. A lack of personal development by the leader

MAJOR OBSTACLE #1: LACK OF UNITY

What is the first thing you think when you hear that a company has co-presidents or dual CEOs?

Many of us immediately think, That isn't going to work. The truth is, it often doesn't. In fact, there are only four Fortune 500 companies with co-CEOs: American Financial Group, KKR, Whole Foods, and, most recently, Oracle. According to Lindred Greer, an assistant professor of organizational behavior at Stanford Graduate School of Business, "The dual-leader setup is rare for a reason" (Zillman 2014). It often gives the two leaders "hostile mind-sets," which causes conflict and results in "negative performance by teams" (Zillman 2014). That doesn't mean it can't be successful. It just means that it rarely is. But why is that?

A dual leader setup can create disunity around vision, and lack of unity around vision is often what leads to division and strife in the business in general. Reaching unity around a vision can be difficult when the power structure is crystal clear, and it can be extremely difficult or even impossible when it isn't. For instance, each leader may have a very different picture of what a high-performing organization will look like. One may envision an organization that produces x number of widgets or x amount of cash. But the other may have a picture that is focused more on the people or creating beautiful products that are easy to use. "High performance" would then mean different things to each leader.

Despite using the same words—*high performance*—the pictures and stories of these two leaders may be completely different. When this happens, and it often does, the result can be destructive. Two competing visions can divide the efforts of employees and dissipate the power of an organization. The word *division* itself gives a stark reminder of the consequences of a split vision—the prefix *di*, after all, means *two* ("Di" n.d.). Two visions = division.

Alternatively, two CEOs can simply result in an out-and-out power struggle. Here's an example from an experience I had early in my consulting career.

I was called by a private equity fund's primary investor to see if I could help their comanaging directors with their leadership, as they were struggling to get along. I wasn't sure if I could help or not, so I asked if I could interview them both and then circle back with my thoughts. The meetings with each of the directors were very tense. One codirector was seething with anger as he described their problems. The other was so distraught he seemed to be in physical pain; he had tears running down his face as he gave me his version of what was going on.

Afterward, I called the investor and shared what I saw. "The problem is you have two heads with different visions. Two visions equals division. The management of your fund is like an animal with two heads, and both heads want to go in a different direction. It isn't going to happen."

I explained that the only way to fix the problem was to choose one person to lead. Unless they took that step, I wouldn't be able to help them; trying to move forward with two leaders would be a waste of time.

I did not get the work. I don't know what eventually happened, but the codirector who had been in tears called me afterward. He agreed that the structure needed to change and said he was trying to find another job.

I think about that story often because it had a huge impact on me. It was my first real understanding of the power of unity and the destructive power of disunity.

1. That particular situation had two leaders tearing the whole apart, but teams can also lack unity, which impacts their ability to contribute to reaching the vision. In another example, Simon once worked with a California team in the consumer appliance industry that had five men and one woman. The CEO brought Simon in to work with his senior team because he couldn't get them on the same page. Simon met with the team and asked them to answer the two questions from Marshall Goldsmith's Team Building without Time Wasting exercise *(www.youtube .com/watch?v=hq2CnccWdPs)*: On a scale of 1 to 10, how well do you believe you are working as a team?

2. On a scale of 1 to 10, how well do you need to be working together to successfully achieve your vision and execute on the strategy?

Everyone wrote down their numbers, and Simon tallied the scores and then put the averages up on the flip chart:

- For the first question, the average was 3.
- For the second question, the average was 8.

At this point, the company was losing money. They had a discussion and learned that the team was lacking trust and competing against each other. Digging a little deeper, Simon discovered that the CEO was unintentionally contributing to their lack of unity. He had from time to time been very aggressive, even yelling at team members who didn't achieve their goals or who made mistakes. The result was that individuals were looking out only for themselves, protecting themselves and their own interests in order to survive. This clearly wasn't helpful for the team.

The CEO received the feedback well and decided to address it openly and with focus. He talked to the team and began to change the way he interacted with them. The team rallied as the CEO changed his behavior, and they all realized they could improve together. Working to improve collectively made a real difference. When Simon asked the same team-building questions one year later, these were the results:

1. On a scale of 1 to 10, how well do you believe you are working as a team? *New answer: 6.6.*

2. On a scale of 1 to 10, how well do you need to be working together to successfully achieve your vision and execute on the strategy? *New answer: 8.*

Their revenues began to improve and they were at a break-even point financially.

When Simon asked them the same question two years later, these were the results:

1. On a scale of 1 to 10, how well do you believe you are working as a team? *New answer: 8.*

2. On a scale of 1 to 10, how well do you need to be working together to successfully achieve your vision and execute on the strategy? *New answer: 8.*

Their revenues had improved significantly, and that year they made $30 million.

Executive Unity, Team Unity, Culture Unity

Companies that succeed place an emphasis on the need for unity throughout the culture. For example, Hilti's impressive culture has been studied by Harvard and has won numerous awards and business accolades. Eivind Slaaen and Dr. Baschera told us that unity starts at the top. When they had a leader who couldn't get aligned with the vision, they made a change in the leader. They created a two-day workshop on culture, and the first ones to go through it were the members of the board, followed by the senior executives. They also built a half-day workshop to roll out the strategy, and this workshop was eventually attended by all 22,000 employees from 120 countries in cohorts of thirty people over a six-month period. And again, guess who did the workshop first? That's right: the board of directors, followed by the senior executives. They aligned at the top of the house first. Then they cascaded the vision, strategy, and culture down through the organization. And to ensure buy-in at every level, they pulled seventy-five managers from throughout the global organization, trained them to be "Sherpas," and had *them* teach the workshops. Throughout the organization, Hilti's leaders take a lot of time and effort to ensure that they have unity: one vision and one team.

Similarly, Rick Anderson at St. Luke's also recognized the need for leaders to fit with the culture. As earlier sections have shown, he quickly took steps to amend the situation after he made the wrong decision when it came to hiring a CFO.

Jack Welch has described a similar experience at GE, where he hired great salespeople who didn't fit within the culture and he had to let them go (Welch and Byrne 2001), and no doubt many other great CEOs have been through something comparable. It takes courage to admit the mistake and put it right, but it demonstrates visionary capability to see that the culture has to be role-modeled from the top. No excuses.

MAJOR OBSTACLE #2: PRECONCEIVED NOTIONS

Getting even two people to share a common picture of the future can be difficult (just think about marriage!), but getting thousands of people to share a common picture is like trying to solve a Rubik's Cube. Just when you think you have it all aligned, one of the six sides has a colored cube in the wrong place.

Leaders who are trying to create a shared vision must first accept that each and every person has his or her own ideas and preconceived notions about what could be and what should be. In order to address this, leaders must give a lot of thought to the way the vision is rolled out and communicated. Before lumberjacks can fell a tree, they must spend time clearing a place for that tree to fall. Then they must cut carefully so that the tree falls where it is supposed to. Leaders can do the same thing when rolling out their vision. It takes a little thought and patience, but it's better to take time to clear a place for the vision to land than to let it settle in an unreceptive or even hostile environment.

Clearing the landing place for the vision means helping employees let go of the past, let go of the current vision and the assumptions about what they think the future of the organization should be. But, unlike felling a tree, landing a vision in the hearts of employees is not a once-and-done thing. Leaders need to be continually clearing and continually working to keep the vision in the hearts of the employees. Leaders can help others lay aside all of the things that get in the way of engaging around a vision by painting the picture clearly so everyone can begin to visualize together. Everyone needs to know where they're going, how they're going to get there, and what part they will play in the story of the vision.

Disarming assumptions involves asking better questions, challenging each other, and challenging ourselves. Leaders can help set the stage by modeling the behavior that is desired all the way through the organization. Leaders who want their employees to challenge their own thinking and become open to experiments and options need to show them how it's done by doing it personally and authentically. Lead by example—we're all familiar with the phrase, but how many of us actually take the time to do it?

MAJOR OBSTACLE #3: LACK OF BUY-IN THROUGH THE ORGANIZATION

Leaders must also address the need to gain buy-in throughout the organization. It's one thing to create a compelling vision and roll it out, but at its best, a vision becomes shared and internalized via deep conversations about how it pertains to the work between senior leaders and staff. As explained earlier, some organizations even engage in hands-on contribution to its creation. This hands-on approach naturally addresses preconceived notions, and not just on the part of staff. As senior leaders test out their vision with employees, they can learn much more about how it applies in real-world situations. To understand this properly, it helps to think about how human beings naturally tend to care about something that they help create. When a person has a say and helps to create a vision, it becomes as much that person's baby as the company's or the small group of people who started the discussion.

Although rarely done in reality, another powerful process is to engage significant portions of employees involved in deep, work-related conversation about the vision. The how-to is a little more complicated. It takes a lot of thought and strategy in the beginning, followed by allocated employee time and resources. Many leaders choose to forgo the effort and revert to a more command-and-control, top-down approach, simply saying to their employees, "Here's our vision; let's go get it." However, while the upfront costs of the more complicated approach may be higher, and it may appear that these conversations will slow things down, in the long run skipping the conversation significantly reduces the odds for success.

In fact, the research says that 70 percent of change initiatives fail. In a study by McKinsey of 1,546 business executives from around the world, only 30 percent agreed that their company's change programs were "completely or mostly" successful (Isern and Pung 2006). Alternatively, success can soar to 79 percent when targeted effort and resources are included. A later McKinsey report explains that "strong leadership and maintaining energy for change among employees are two principles of success that reinforce each other when executed well. When leaders ensure that frontline staff members feel a sense of ownership, the results show a 70 percent success rate for transformations. When frontline employees take the initiative to drive change, transformations have a 71 percent success rate. When both principles are used, the success rate rises to 79 percent" (Keller, Meaney, and Pung 2010).

This is a critical piece of insight. Because vision is key to transformation, John, Simon, and I decided to talk to someone who specialized in gaining buy-in for transformational change: Bruce A. Strong of CBridge Partners. Bruce is the coauthor, along with J.-C. Spender, of *Strategic Conversations: Creating and Directing the Entrepreneurial Workforce* (2014). Considering our quest to engage employees and in particular the emerging Gen Y, who we know to be more difficult to engage with, we knew we were on the right track. During our interview, Bruce explained the success/failure percentages we mentioned earlier.

"Organizational hierarchies are good for accountability but not very good for communication. That goes for both communication going down and communication coming up. Let's just take the business model as an example. Organizations need to continuously innovate their business model, but in order to do that, leaders need knowledge, and the more knowledge they have, the better. If they are just listening to the senior leaders, they are missing at least 80 percent of the organization, and that 80 percent are the ones closest to the work and the customer. Instead, to change effectively, businesses need to create a strategic conversation, one that gets all of the parts communicating and innovating at the same time."

Bruce shared some examples of this with us:

1. **Vision Creation:** Red Hat, a global provider of open source, enterprise IT solutions based in Raleigh, North Carolina, is perhaps the most radical practitioner of these types of conversations. They opened up the vision to the entire company. They put a half-baked vision on LISTSERV and asked the employees to join the conversation. The employees engaged. The leaders began a conversation that ultimately culminated in a shared vision. The employees bought in to the vision because they helped create it, and they did it in their own old-school, open-platform, techie way.

2. **Competition:** KBS (Kirshenbaum Bond Senecal + partners), a New York City–based creative agency, wanted to have a strategic conversation with employees about how to reach their vision. They created a competition and asked employees what ideas they had that would deliver this goal. One of the ideas was to develop a lab for testing ideas. They called it Hyde Space. Like Dr. Jekyll and Mr. Hyde, it would have two roles: Dr. Jekyll during the day would

do regular work, but by night, Mr. Hyde would test the craziest of ideas. By doing this, the company created a space where their vision could, at once, be realized and refined. Every time work happened in Hyde Space, employees were working collectively and experimentally to simultaneously achieve and develop their corporate vision. Hyde Space has become the literal and figurative heart of the organization and it is felt at all levels.

3. **T-Shaped Conversations** (Hansen 2009): EMC is a very large and global data storage, information security, and cloud-computing company headquartered in Hopkinton, Massachusetts. They involve their top 150 executives in a strategic conversation based on the idea that business unit leaders' focus needs to be T-shaped. In other words, the leaders need to be experts in their business unit but also take responsibility for the overall success of the organization (Spender and Strong 2014). The CEO said that every fifteen years or so, the company changes radically, and he wanted to know what they needed to change now to be successful in the future. By examining this issue, EMC leaders begin to think much more broadly and systematically about the company, and a natural buy-in to the emerging vision arises.

4. **Innovation Communities:** The New York Public Library has nearly 51 million items and serves more than 17 million patrons per year ("About the New York Public Library" 2016). The chief library officer, Mary Lee Kennedy, established three innovation communities to work on creating the organization's vision: reference, circulation, and collections. The innovation communities were tasked with coming up with option statements that they would present to senior management on how they could achieve the vision. The vision statement had to be included in the option statement. That created a lot of conversation about how to achieve the vision and included multiple layers of people reaching down into the workforce, the part of the organization closest to its work and its patrons.

The first layer of each community included a small group of employees (five to seven) who were dedicated full-time to the task during the project. Since there were three communities, that meant a total of approximately fifteen dedicated staff members. The second layer was a group of 150 testers. This group operated like a start-up and tested the ideas out in the workplace. The third layer included anyone in the organization who wanted to participate in conversations about how to implement the vision. (About 250 people ultimately took part in this offer.) Thus a significant portion of the 2,500-plus-member workforce was now talking about, thinking about, and, ultimately, working on achieving the vision.

When vision is at the heart of strategic conversations within organizations, it is extremely powerful.

Bruce's work highlights that when vision is at the heart of strategic conversations within organizations, it is extremely powerful in gaining buy-in and creating the energy to move the vision forward. This kind of ownership is exactly what is required in the modern world. As power shifts to the emerging workforce, those deep in the organization will need to have much more information than organizational leaders are used to sharing.

When an entire workforce is a part of the process that creates the vision for the company, they are more compelled to achieve it, and the company profits in the long run. Their collective brains come together to create an achievable and assertive strategy within a given time frame. They clearly understand the values, including the ways in which they will and will not achieve the vision, and they understand the intent of their leaders. In other words, employees on the front line are so well informed they can make decisions independently, with relative certainty that the organizational leaders approve of them. The right intent in everyday decision making on the front line flows directly from the overarching vision, through the implementation of strategy and a shared set of values.

If vision, strategy, and values are well implemented and understood, leaders can feel secure in empowering employees to make decisions at the point closest to the need. Leaders then become more focused on checking for alignment, rather than micromanaging the day-to-day actions of their staff.

Feedback-rich Culture Is a Way to Foster Empowerment and Alignment

Empowering employees effectively works best in a feedback-rich culture. Fortunately, it's becoming easier to manage this kind of program every day. Our society now uses instant feedback on almost everything through a variety of digital tools. If you book a restaurant or hotel online, you will often receive an email or SMS the following day wanting to hear your views on the experience. Order a product and let the retailer know your cell number and you'll get regular updates, including when the product was delivered. Even cars that are built with wireless technology are constantly feeding back data to the manufacturer. However, feedback for empowerment and alignment with a vision still requires some old-school communication skills. Leaders need to make the time to think about how to help those close to the customer and work out a way to communicate feedback to employees that is helpful and not hurtful. The better and more well-thought-out the feedback process, the greater the impact will be on helping its recipient improve and progress. Here are a few tips for giving feedback to support empowerment and alignment with the vision:

- **Make feedback genuine.** As we shared in the earlier section about courage through vulnerability, humans are really good at picking up on the true intentions behind any message. This is true whether it's communicated through language or nonverbal cues such as tone or body language. So, the intention behind the feedback must always stem from a genuine desire to serve the person who is receiving the feedback, and it must be delivered in a sincere and supportive way. If it isn't, employees will be less likely to take it to heart and use it to improve performance.

- **Understand that feedback is *subjective*.** Feedback involves the deliverer's interpretation of a behavior and the recipient's interpretation of the deliverer's intentions. The experience of the recipient will determine the success or lack of success in their desire to improve.

  It helps to think through and pay close attention to language signals used during feedback. Using phrases such as "I think" or "I noticed" conveys to receivers that the observation about their performance is subjective and isn't intended as an indictment. "I" language encourages open dialogue between givers and receivers, which allows both sides to better address the issue without defensiveness or malice.

  When recipients understand that they are hearing an opinion, they have room to save face and be more receptive to change. They hear, "This is my story. It may help you, but I could be wrong, so you have to evaluate it for yourself." Even when leaders are sure they are right, insisting that a person change isn't the best approach most of the time. Instead, leaders may want to consider offering ideas and suggestions, simply allowing the receiver to decide what to do with it.

- **Deliver feedback in the moment (or soon after).** Feedback is almost always most effective when it is delivered immediately following the behavior or situation. According to an Achiever's Intelligence poll, over 60 percent of employees like to receive immediate "on-the-spot" feedback from their managers ("Achievers" 2012). This allows employees the opportunity to immediately change their behavior and then be recognized for it, which will lead to higher engagement and a higher sense of motivation ("Achievers" 2012).

- **The goal of feedback is encouraging excellence—not causing embarrassment.** Nobody wants to be belittled or treated with condescension. It's counterproductive and a morale killer. The best feedback is given in a respectful way and in the context of an employee's positive contributions to the organization.

- **Start with the assumption that you'll learn something.** Of course you can give feedback but you want to receive it too. If someone wants to give feedback to you, then make the time to listen, because that person could be waiting to tell you how the service you just launched isn't going down well with the customer. Alignment works both ways, and sometimes the strategy needs to flex just as much as the team.

MAJOR OBSTACLE #4: A LACK OF URGENCY

In order to achieve a shared vision, a sense of urgency must be established. This is big. Without a sense of urgency, the shared vision isn't going to happen. Why not? Well, let's just think about human nature for a moment. Most people do not decide to eat healthily until they are either overweight or sick. They don't get serious about a career change until their job is threatened. It's just human nature. Whatever the urgent tasks are from day to day, they will grab our attention, and the long-term important things will get pushed to the back burner. So the only way to achieve a common vision with a large group of people is to paint the clear picture and engage others in a way that connects their heart to the vision. At this point everyone needs to agree how the team will and will not go about achieving the vision. Finally, leaders need to set assertive goals and actions. The goals must be challenging, but they also need to be possible to reach within a specific time frame.

Establishing assertive time lines is important because that sets the tone for urgency. Time lines that are too aggressive lead to excessive stress, and time lines that are not aggressive enough lead to complacency. If leaders go too fast, then people feel out of control; if they go too slow then it feels like nothing is actually changing. In order to achieve the right balance, leaders need to take the time to think through time lines, ensuring the end dates are assertive and yet achievable with some hustle.

Of course, reaching for a compelling vision, though an incredibly positive process, often requires change, and change makes people nervous. Channel that nervous energy into productivity and results, just as jockeys channel the nervous energy of their horses into the power to win the race.

Sprinting for a long season is not possible, but going after something wholeheartedly for a long season is. Building in a sense of urgency is an important part of the process. There will always be obstacles, major and minor, but what matters is to meet each challenge in turn, to stay optimistic, and to keep moving forward.

At the very beginning of this book, we talked about the road covered in fog. For many people, that is what change can feel like: they simply can't see the road far ahead enough to feel comfortable. This is why communication and feedback are key. People want to know that progress is being made; it spurs them on and lets them know that what they are doing is right. That's when the fog starts to lift and the road becomes clearer.

MAJOR OBSTACLE #5: A LACK OF PERSONAL DEVELOPMENT BY THE LEADER

Leading with vision ultimately doesn't work unless there is a leader. Effective leaders will impact the process from beginning to end. These leaders must buy in and demonstrate leadership of the vision, the workforce, and of themselves. A lack of self-awareness or a lack of personal commitment to growing leadership skills can derail otherwise effective strategies to reach the vision.

When employees interact with a CEO or other top leader, they have an experience. That experience is either positive or negative. Every time leaders interact with their staff, they can ask themselves, I wonder how that experience was for them? What am I like to work with?

This question helps leaders revisit the encounter and think through what went well and what didn't go well. The more leaders are willing to look at themselves and improve, the better the leadership experience others will receive. This goes back to our earlier discussion about being courageous enough to be vulnerable as a leader. Let's review a few case studies drawn from my coaching sessions with a few of my clients to see how their experiences reflect this.[1]

Anne: From Strength to Liability

Anne had just been promoted to operations manager for the U.S. West Coast region of a global technology company. Previously she was responsible for 50 people. With this promotion, she was in charge of operations with 150 people, providing operational support and service for customers. Her company brought in a coach to support her in transitioning into her new role with bigger responsibilities. She was charged with leading her division, executing the strategy, and helping to achieve the overall vision of her company.

When her coach sat down with Anne, he asked about her current work situation. She said,

> "I love my job. I am passionate about it and I love to solve problems. I believe I am good at what I do. But I have no personal life and no balance. I work about seventy-five hours each week. I come in early in the morning, leave late, and also work on weekends. I don't have a life anymore."

Her facial expression showed high levels of stress and anxiety. She was definitely overwhelmed, almost burned out, and at a point where she was desperate for help.

After her coach conducted a round of interviews with her coworkers to better understand how they perceived Anne and her leadership, the

---

[1] The following three stories are drawn from coaching clients; identifying details have been changed or removed.

message was loud and clear. It revealed Anne's challenge in her leadership role.

She was a great problem solver, just as she had said. So when managers came to her with a problem, what did she do? She solved it. She took on the task and dove into the details to get it fixed. The next time those managers had a problem, what did they do? They went to Anne again, because they knew she would solve it for them.

Based on this feedback, Anne realized her problematic behavioral pattern. She allowed her managers to come to her with problems instead of empowering and enabling them to solve the problems themselves.

Anne was overwhelmed with the numerous projects and problems she handled. She was very tactical and neglected her role to lead and set direction. She didn't have the time to guide her managers to lead their teams. She was in the trees and couldn't see the forest. Her biggest strength, solving problems, had become her biggest liability.

With this data and new insight, she was able to take action and change her behaviors. She went back to her coworkers, thanked them for the feedback, and said, "In my new expanded leadership role, I would like to elicit your help. I want to get better at coaching my managers, support them in their role, and hold them accountable for the results we have to deliver. Will you please help me?"

Those words to her coworkers were initially very uncomfortable for Anne. But it did not demonstrate weakness; it demonstrated her courage. Anne was vulnerable and took the risk to fully engage her coworkers and allow them to support her in her role. She was willing to see and address the behavior that was inhibiting her growth.

After this, Anne diligently focused on her own self-improvement. She also worked on empowering her team and helping them develop their own problem-solving skills. She coached her managers on a monthly basis and then provided support and guidance. As a result, she reaped tremendous benefits and peace of mind. At the end of her coaching engagement, she had delivered all of her business targets. She received another promotion and is now leading 300 people. She now works an average of 60 hours a week instead of 70, and on the weekends, she goes riding with her husband on their Harley.

Bill: The Drive to Be the Perfect CEO

Bill took on a new position as CEO of an aerospace manufacturing company. The company, which had been family-owned for more than thirty years, had recently been bought by a private equity group at a low price. The company faced major business challenges. Product quality was low, and they missed deliverables to their clients. Their systems and processes were outdated. Bill was brought in to turn the company around because of his reputation as a driven, ambitious, and demanding executive. The vision was to turn the company around and create a profitable and ultimately sellable organization.

The human resource manager brought in a coach to conduct a few team and leadership development workshops with Bill and nine of his direct reports. Very quickly the coach saw the picture and problem emerging. Bill, knowledgeable and determined to fix the company problems, spent most of his time on the production floor, telling the assembly line workers how to do their jobs. He was action-oriented, with high-performance expectations for himself and others, but he soon became impatient and constantly dissatisfied with everyone around him. Nothing was fast enough or good enough. He failed to appreciate and motivate his team. Instead of engaging and empowering his managers, he disengaged and disempowered them.

The team coach met with Bill and offered him individual coaching. The coach was eager and certain he could help Bill make some behavioral modifications that would help him build his team and get back on track. Unfortunately, Bill was not willing and open. He declined the coach's help because he felt that he knew better. He wanted to be perfect, to show the private equity owners he could do it. He lacked a sense of humility or modesty. He certainly wasn't willing to appear vulnerable.

Eventually, the private equity team brought in another CEO to try to clean up the mess. Bill had derailed and failed.

The challenge with vulnerability is that it is often the first thing we as human beings look for in other people and yet it is the last thing we want to show of ourselves. That is where leaders can fall into the "perfection" trap. There is an internal, habitually unconscious voice in all of us that whispers, You are not good enough. Perfectionism is rooted in fear. It tries to give us a sense of control and becomes, at its core, an attempt to earn approval and acceptance. It is self-focused. It is a constantly paranoid voice that keeps asking, What will others think of me?

Bill wanted to be perfect and get approval from the investor team. Yet he failed, because he was not willing to be authentic in his leadership. He was afraid to go to his team and say, "I cannot do this by myself. I need help." This type of language was not in Bill's vocabulary, because he considered it a weakness. In reality it would have been perceived as courage by his colleagues, but he missed the opportunity to connect with his people and infuse much-needed trust in the organization.

Not asking for help is one of the biggest downfalls of leaders, and it is one that will stop leaders from engaging others around a compelling vision. The vision may be there, but if the leaders aren't willing to admit that they can't do it alone, others will not want to come along with them. On the other hand, those who are willing to show their vulnerable side can form a human bond with their team and create the foundation for an engaged and trusted workforce.

Clayton: The Smartest Guy in the Room

A leading sports equipment brand brought in an executive coach for their head of marketing, Clayton. He was leading a team of twenty people. He was driven, he was well-intended, and he desired the best outcome for the organization. Additionally, Clayton was incredibly smart, always ten steps ahead of a problem. He was one of those people who can work out very complex issues in his head and come up with sound solutions.

But interestingly, his intelligence had become the biggest liability in his leadership role. His coach noticed this during one of their coaching sessions. The coach started to give him some leadership advice, but in the middle of his sentence, Clayton cut him off and finished his sentence for him. The coach soon learned that this was what he was doing routinely with all his employees.

The coach decided to do some interviews and obtained feedback from fifteen stakeholders, which confirmed this behavior and its effects on those he led. Although highly intelligent, Clayton was a horrible listener. He always had to show people how smart he was. In fact, he was known as the "know-it-all guy." This leadership style affected everything. Team meetings were unproductive; they lacked creativity and a free flow of ideas because the top guy always had the "answer." His people became disengaged and unmotivated, because their ideas were not heard or acted upon. So, after a few conversations, they finally said, "Why should I bring my ideas? Clayton always knows better than me." Morale was very low, and there was a real concern that people were leaving and taking their ideas with them.

Clayton listened to his coach. He said that he understood, and he acknowledged the feedback He went to his colleagues and said, courageously, "I am sorry that I have not been listening to you. I am willing to make changes. I will improve."

It took him a while, but eventually he stopped needing to show that he was the smartest guy in the room. He learned how to be a better listener, to be more understanding, and to let other people finish their thoughts before he responded. After about six months, one of Clayton's managers said, "It's amazing! Our marketing meetings have become so much better because he doesn't do all the talking."

The team became more innovative, more creative, and more effective. People were more motivated and engaged because they were *heard*. Clayton himself said, "You know what? I don't have to work so hard! I let people talk more so I can manage more effectively. They like it better, and so do I. Now we can help drive strategy and work toward the company vision together."

WHEN A STRENGTH BECOMES A LIABILITY

There are some key questions that leaders can ask themselves to make sure that they are not derailing their ability to lead with vision and engage a workforce. These questions are designed to help leaders step back and expand their ability to see the view that others see. Ultimately, these questions can help leaders develop an awareness of how their behaviors impact others.

- How do I come across?
- What is my emotional impact?
- Does my behavior empower and inspire—or the opposite?
- How do I know when my behaviors add value or create a risk?
- What are my potential derailers (behaviors—often unconscious ones—that limit or reduce leadership effectiveness)?
- How do I show courage and vulnerability without coming across weak?

A lack of self-awareness is a problem for leading with vision, but it isn't an inborn trait that can't be fixed. Leaders can get support to become better at their jobs and to correct leadership problems. They can learn to deliver powerful messages that come from the heart, from a place of passion.

In order to touch others in a compelling way, great leaders have to understand who they are. Self-awareness also plays a very important role in our next topic: communicating in a way that moves people.

TAKEAWAYS FROM CHAPTER 9

- **The research shows that in most cases, just a few types of obstacles are responsible for preventing the creation and implementation of compelling corporate visions.** Once leaders understand what these are, and their role in creating or maintaining them, they can devise strategies to overcome them.
    1. Create unity
    2. Challenge preconceived notions
    3. Gain buy-in down through the organization
    4. Establish an appropriate sense of urgency
    5. Encourage personal development for every leader

- **Leaders can use the lessons of others to improve their own performance.** It's useful to consider how the behavior of leaders we have all encountered have created obstacles in realizing the vision of the organizations they've led. Equally, the stories of how similar obstacles have been overcome can provide real inspiration for our own personal development and growth as leaders.

- **Self-awareness is a key factor in helping leaders successfully build and communicate a vision.** There are some key questions that all leaders can ask themselves to make sure that they are not derailing their ability to lead with vision and engage a workforce.

CHAPTER 10

Professor or Poet?

CONNECTING WITH EMOTIONS

"I HAVE A DREAM THAT MY FOUR LITTLE CHILDREN will one day live in a nation where. . ."

"Ask not what your country can do for you. . ."

"If not you, then. . ."

Most of us can finish these famous lines. They are quotes that have inspired millions to take action. Why? Because they move us. They touch something inside of us. They connect with our emotions.

While most leaders agree that creating a compelling vision for the future is crucial, many of these same leaders struggle with the idea of reaching employees at an emotional level. We hear statements like "I'm not an emotional leader." "I want our employees to operate on logic, not feelings." "I'm going to appeal to their brains, not their emotions." It's as if emotions are an insult to intelligence. But nothing could be further from the truth.

While most leaders agree that creating a compelling vision for the future is crucial, many of these same leaders struggle with the idea of reaching employees at an emotional level.

The research is vast and compelling. Today, many psychologists argue that emotions are the dominant driver of the most meaningful life decisions.

The research of Jennifer Lerner and her colleagues, published in their 2015 paper, concluded that "emotion and decision making go hand in hand" (804). In fact, their research has one overarching conclusion: "Emotions powerfully, predictably, and pervasively influence decision making" (804).

Marketers have known this for some time. OluKai's marketing imagery is all designed to stimulate an emotional connection between the customer and the product; it's core to everything they do. In a paper called "The Role of Emotions in Marketing" (Bagozzi, Gopinath, and Nyer 1999), the authors state, "A person's emotional state can influence various aspects of information processing including encoding and retrieval of information, different strategies used to process information, evaluations and judgments and creative thinking."

They go on to say, "Sometimes emotions spur one into action; at other times emotions inhibit or constrain action." They also describe how marketers use this knowledge to tap into consumers' emotions with goal-oriented products such as diet plans. Balancing the positive emotions of losing weight with the negative emotions of not losing weight spurs people into action, and the more messages they receive, the more engaged they become. The research showed that "the anticipatory emotions then energized volitions in the form of intentions, plans and decisions to expend energy in the service of goal striving."

Isn't this what every leader wants to achieve? People motivated and making plans to achieve a shared goal? Of course it is, which is why we want our leaders to tell us stories rather than give lectures; we want poets, not professors.

Assuming we have convinced you, the next questions may be, "So what? What do we do with this information?" Well, in light of what we are trying to accomplish here, we can use this information in two ways.

1. Use emotion to create the compelling vision.
2. Use emotion to communicate the compelling vision and engage others around it.

Before wrinkling your nose at the thought, remember: the research is clear. Any time in history that a great vision has been achieved, it has been because a group of individuals chose collectively to strive to achieve it. That collective choice has almost always been primarily driven by emotion.

But how? How do leaders use emotion as a method for engaging employees? Well, honestly, through a bit of romance, poetry, and maybe even a little drama.

THE PROFESSOR TURNED POET

Think back to your university professors. Some probably rattled off statistics and facts like *Star Trek's* Lieutenant Commander Data without regard to the notion that there were actual humans listening to them. Type in "the most boring lecture ever" into Google. The first page of results is full of videos uploaded by disengaged, and sometimes quite angry, audience members.

> *Some professors captivate their students. They are more like poets than professors.*

On the other hand, some professors captivate their students. They make the information they have to impart, whatever it is, come to life. They make it breathe, they make it personal, and their students eat it up. They are more like poets than professors. Their classes are always full, and their students arrive early at registration and scramble for position to make sure that they are able to get on the roster. Word spreads through the student grapevine that this professor is the best.

This was epitomized in the 1989 film *Dead Poets Society* (*Dead* 1989). In the film, the late Robin Williams played a schoolteacher, John Keating, who had an unorthodox but very effective method of engaging with his students and making his classes more exciting. Of course, his more uptight colleagues didn't approve of his style, but he achieved results. At one point Keating stood at the front of his class, all fired up, and declared: "We don't read and write poetry because it's cute. We read and write poetry because we are members of the human race. And the human race is filled with passion. And medicine, law, business, engineering, these are noble pursuits and necessary to sustain life. But poetry, beauty, romance, love, these are what we stay alive for." Those three last sentences are more applicable today than they have ever been; they could have been written for Generation Y.

I used to have a great professor, and he used to tell us a story about a class he attended when he was a student. It's a story that's stayed with me all these years.

My professor used to be a football player, back in the day, and he and his friends would often skip class, fool around, or take a nap in the back row of their classes. But one afternoon, in a three-hour history lesson, something happened that changed all this.

"This particular day," he said, "we all came in with our usual attitude, joking around, sleepy, bored. Some of us leaned back in our chairs, some put our head on our hands, some flirted with the nearby girls, and some pulled out a notebook to at least pretend to take notes.

"Our professor was late. He was never late. But today was different. Instead of him being at the front of the room as he usually was when students rolled in, he entered the room from the side five minutes after class was supposed to start. He was dressed sharply, perhaps a little more tailored than usual. He held a paper in his hands, and slowly at first, he began to speak. He was giving a speech, a very good speech. The students, including the football players, all began to pay attention. This wasn't just a good speech. It was a great speech, and he was delivering it with extreme prowess. The students leaned forward. They started to take notes. They listened with rapt attention. At the end of his speech, he paused and stood, silent for a moment. Then the students began to clap; then they began to stand. Eventually the entire class was giving this Friday afternoon history teacher a standing ovation. It went on for a long time. As the applause eventually died down, the professor took the speech he had in his hand and slammed it on the podium. Then he spoke the word that reverberated through the class: 'Hitler!'"

He had just read a speech by Hitler, and the unknowing students had been so emotionally moved that they gave it a standing ovation. Why? Because Hitler knew how to move people emotionally. He knew the power of the spoken word and how to get people to do incredible—and, in his case, unspeakable—things.

None of us wants to be like Hitler, of course, but that's not the point. The point is that words are powerful. They are extremely powerful. They can hurt. They can inspire. They can move people to perform feats they never dreamt they were capable of.

PAINTING THE PICTURE

Words can bring things to life. Even a vision, even a company, can become more powerful and more meaningful when it becomes connected to our hearts through words.

In 2013, Inc.com ran an article on the worst company vision and mission statements. This was number three: "To create a shopping experience that pleases our customers; a workplace that creates opportunities and a great working environment for our associates; and a business that achieves financial success" (Zetlin 2013). You could replace "a shopping" with just "an" and that statement could apply to every business in the world. And most likely the people who work for this organization know it. There's nothing compelling or aspirational or emotional here. It's hard to imagine a room full of people hearing this for the first time and thinking, "This will get me taking the stairs two steps at a time tomorrow."

By way of contrast, this is the vision statement for Save the Children: "Our vision is a world in which every child attains the right to survival, protection, development and participation." This is a vision that's easy to build a story around, and it absolutely connects with people emotionally. I mean, who wouldn't agree with that statement? It's clear about what they want to achieve and the specific work they need to do; their staff and volunteers can immediately see their role in the bigger picture.

The vision itself is important, but so is the way it is communicated.

The vision itself is important, but so is the way it is communicated. As a leader, it will, at some point, be your responsibility to stand up and take ownership of the vision through a speech or presentation to others. How you convey the vision, the passion with which you bring it alive for the people, your ability to visualize the better future that you're working toward, and the emotions this will create—all of these will be on your shoulders.

Knowing how to do this technically is important, of course, and there are hundreds of books on presentation skills that will tell you that you need to be relaxed, maintain eye contact, use hand gestures, speak at a moderate pace; on and on the list goes. But there is more. There are deeper ways in which you can connect with your employees. Those ways include the following:

- **Be authentic.** Nobody is buying into a vision that you don't believe in.

- **Show passion.** Role-modeling behavior starts here. If you're passionate, then others will be.

- **Speak to your audience.** Don't write one general speech and repeat it over and over; speak to each audience as if you're talking for the first time, and make it relevant to them.

- **Share your visualization.** We don't book holidays based on textual descriptions; we imagine ourselves sitting next to the pool. We can see ourselves in the picture.

- **Be clear about expectations.** If you want people to change, tell them, and tell them why.

- **Show vulnerability.** Even just saying, "I can't do it without you," will strike a chord.

- **Be supportive.** If you're asking people to change, then tell them that you understand it will be hard, and explain how you will be helping them to adapt.
- **Focus on the goal.** That is what the vision is, after all.

SAY IT LIKE YOU MEAN IT, LIKE YOUR LIFE DEPENDS ON IT

Many years ago I stumbled across a book in the famous Brattle Bookstore in Boston. The book was published in the 1920s, and I was drawn to the title, *Loyalty in Business*. It was written by Elbert Hubbard, a writer, artist, and philosopher, and it contains a series of essays on how to succeed in business (Hubbard 1921). I haven't read it for years now, but it is still on my shelf, and I still have a quote, taken from the book, that I scrawled on a notepad: "Don't try to eliminate the old-fashioned virtues—many have tried it, with indifferent success. No good substitute has yet been found for simplicity, frankness, sobriety, industry and sincerity. To think, to see, to feel, to know, to deal justly; to bear all patiently, to act quietly; to speak cheerfully; to moderate one's voice—these things will bring you the highest good." The language may be dated, but the spirit of what Hubbard is saying is still true today; the "highest good"—that's your vision. "To think, to see, to feel, to know"; that is precisely what the leaders we have met throughout this book have been telling us.

Remember also that the first time you share the vision, you need to bring people along. It helps if the vision has been a collaborative effort, but the likelihood is that there are still plenty who will need to buy in to it. To a certain extent, you're pitching, and Hubbard's advice about simplicity is correct.

Here's an example from a film pitch. The film *Alien* runs for almost two hours, and it has a cast of eight main characters (*Alien* 2004). I recently read a synopsis of the film that ran for more than 540 words. It was thorough, detailed, factual—and slightly dull. The pitch to the movie studio was just three words: "*Jaws* in space." It was visual, emotional, and simple; it provided clarity. It's poetry. It's not a call to action in the same way that a vision is, but if you can apply the same creative thinking to simplifying and visualizing your message, then you have a greater chance of making a connection with the audience.

Perhaps the most inspirational person in the field of presentations has been Richard Saul Wurman, the "designer" of the TED conferences. After attending multiple conferences in the 1980s, Wurman was desperate for a different format—something that was inspirational and connected the speaker and the audience—so he subtracted. In a video he told *Smithsonian* magazine, "I subtracted panels of white men in suits, CEOs and politicians, lecterns, introductions and I subtracted long speeches" ("Creator of TED Conference" 2012). Then he went further and subtracted presentations and time. Wurman wanted speakers to get to the point, to find ways to connect, and to make people pay attention and listen. If a speaker like Prosanta Chakrabarty (2016) can present the clues to prehistoric times found in blind cavefish in under five minutes, how long should it really take to describe a vision?

Wurman wanted speakers to get to the point, to find ways to connect, and to make people pay attention and listen.

Wurman sold TED many years ago, but the format he created still survives and thrives today. The eighteen-minute presentation, often without any presentation support, is popular across the world and has spawned a number of similar conferences. The TED format has taught presenters to think like poets and not like professors. TED.com has more than 2,200 talks, but we are pretty sure they are still waiting for someone to talk about leading with vision!

ARISTOTLE: THE POETICS

Aristotle was a pupil of Plato in fourth-century B.C. Athens, and in 335 B.C. he wrote *The Poetics*, which was the first writing on literary criticism

(Aristotle 1968). He referred to the material as *poetics* because at that time oratory was the main form of communication. Storytelling was common, and in order for someone to be able to share a story, that person needed to remember it, so stories were created with a rhythm—a poetry that could be remembered—and that's the way that stories, philosophies, and history spread.

In *The Poetics*, Aristotle critiqued the works of playwrights and philosophers, and he identified common techniques for structure and devices for creating drama. His greatest gift to writers was recognizing that narrative has a beginning, a middle, and an end.

This structure is still used today in movie writing, and it is commonly taught at school for composing essays. In the movies, they refer to it as the "three-act script," and each act is roughly the same length. In fact, if we want to think more like poets than like professors, we will want to consider how we structure our message and keep the right balance with a beginning, a middle, and an end.

Perhaps the most disciplined form of the "three acts" is Japanese haiku. Take, for example, the sixteenth-century poet Matsuo Basho (Beilenson 1962):

An old silent pond . . .
A frog jumps into the pond,
splash! Silence again.

This is a visual story: it's poetic, engaging, and clear, with a beginning, a middle, and an end.

BECOMING A POET

Writing poetry may be out of your comfort zone, but I hope that by now you are convinced of the need to engage people emotionally, find connections in your message, and think about your message as a story rather than an academic lecture. I would recommend looking through the great speeches of our time and considering how the writer follows this advice:

Thread the theme. Identify your theme, which could be culture, service, collaboration, change, or any variant of these topics. Know what your theme is, and ensure that you thread it through the narrative. Make it explicit. Join the dots for the audience; don't make them work to understand what it is you're trying to convey.

Use the power of three. The rule of three or the power of three is a proven device for effective writing and speaking. A list of three points has a rhythm but is also memorable. To list five points risks the danger or one or more being forgotten.

Balance the long and the short. Where long sentences are necessary, follow them with short sentences. Professors are known for writing and delivering long sentences; audience members, waiting for the point, soon forget how the sentence started and then their mind wanders. Use short sentences to punctuate your points and maintain engagement with your audience. It's often the shorter sentences that are packed with emotion.

Move the story on. Once you've made your point, move on. Trust that you have gotten your message across. Nobody wants to hear the same point rephrased six times.

End with poetry. You don't have to literally write or read a poem, but you may want to find a way to encapsulate your message and any key themes in one last sentence or phrase. Create, through your words, a moment of clarity, and remember that your last phrase is what the audience will first remember.

Leading with vision requires skills, and while the oratory and writing skills needed to captivate employees around a vision may not come naturally, they can be learned. Rhetoric is "the art or skill of speaking or writing formally and effectively especially as a way to persuade or influence people."

With a little thought and practice, all leaders can learn to use the poetic, the romantic, the dramatic, and other forms of rhetoric in their business life. In fact, there are many tools that can be added to your toolbox as a leader and influencer. Here are just a few of the rhetorical devices, with definitions taken from *Merriam-Webster*, which may come in handy.

- **Anecdote:** a usually short narrative of an interesting, amusing, or biographical incident (covered more thoroughly in our chapter on storytelling).
- **Aphorism:** a short phrase that expresses a true or wise idea. Example: "If it ain't broke, don't fix it."
- **Contradiction:** a difference or disagreement between two things, which means that both cannot be true. Example: A tall midget.
- **Hyperbole:** language that describes something as better or worse than it really is. Example: "I've told you a million times."
- **Imagery:** language that causes people to imagine pictures in their mind. Example: "I stepped out of my Jeep Wrangler at the plant. The sun was hot and in my eyes, and I hesitated before walking across the gravel."
- **Litotes:** an understatement in which an affirmative is expressed by the negative of the contrary. Example: "She's not a bad cook."
- **Paradox:** something (such as a situation) that is made up of two opposite things and that seems impossible but is actually true or possible. Example: "I can resist anything but temptation" (Oscar Wilde).

You get the point. People are often more inspired and motivated by the spoken word than by the written word. Language is a powerful tool to reach people. The more leaders focus on improving their communication skills, the better they will be at engaging employees, customers, and partners in their vision. We continue this theme in the next chapter on storytelling.

TAKEAWAYS FROM CHAPTER 10

- Reflect on a time when you had to deliver a key message—what emotions were your audience experiencing and did you tap into them?

- Look back at a recent presentation you have given—does it have a beginning, middle, and end? If not how would you restructure it?
- If you had to deliver the core message of the presentation in three words, what would they be?
- Learn to use rhetorical tools and develop your own skills as a communicator and poet.

CHAPTER 11

Storytelling

A LONG THE LINES OF NEEDING to communicate powerfully and emotionally in order to engage others around a vision, we noted that in all of the cases we had studied, a compelling vision involved more than just words; there was always a story behind it. Whether it was the Jimbo's vision for a piece of organic fruit for every child in a recycled lunch bag or OluKai's vision of a Hawaiian dream that was reflected in everything they did, or OGE's vision to protect the customer's bill, the ability of the leaders to tell those stories and explain what lay behind the vision then created followers out of employees and led to success. In short, those leaders were great storytellers.

Great leaders tell stories to create followers.

Why is it that storytellers, people who are masterful communicators, are so important to leading with vision? The answer is simple: they are the ones who put things in motion. They set off a chain reaction that propels the company forward, enabling it to grow beyond the ordinary to become truly great. Despite this simple truth, however, our experience of leaders and leadership consistently reveals conflicting priorities. As mentioned earlier, it is often the case that leaders tend to focus on the immediate priorities of making money, meeting customers' needs, resolving problems, and managing processes and people. Leaders are often very effective at managing for today but less effective at preparing for tomorrow. In fact, leaders are especially less effective and focused on the art of storytelling because it is something that takes time, careful thought, creativity, energy, and passion. We highlighted this in the research in chapter 4, where the personal development priorities and business leadership priorities differed greatly; creating a vision and engaging others topped the list of leadership needs, but it fell to the bottom of the list when it came to executive development priorities for the next two or three years.

This is despite the fact that the defining role of leaders is the ability to set the right course and then *take people with them*, with the result that the business develops, competes, and succeeds. Leading with vision means changing—or transforming—the organization so that it can move in a determined way in the right direction. That is a vital challenge that relies on one thing above all others: the ability to communicate in a way that energizes and moves people, activating the heart and hands as well as the head.

Roger Schank (1995), the author of *Tell Me a Story: Narrative and Intelligence*, summed up the challenge facing most leaders: "Humans are not ideally set up to understand logic; they are ideally set up to understand stories." What does Roger mean? Well, for thousands of years human beings communicated orally; people told stories. Even when writing became a popular medium, the Greek philosopher Socrates famously spurned it; he claimed it led to forgetfulness and a pretense of understanding rather than true understanding, which is what he achieved through dialogue with his pupils (Plato 2009).

---

*"Humans are not ideally set up to understand logic;
they are ideally set up to understand stories."*

—Roger Schank

Oral communication continued to dominate until very recently. Even though mass printing has been around for more than 500 years, the majority of most populations were still illiterate until about 150 years ago. Today email dominates as the method of communication in many organizations. According to research from Radicati, over 205 billion emails were sent per day in 2015, and they expect that figure to rise to 246 billion emails per day by 2019 ("Email Statistics Report" 2015). The question is, are they communicating "logic" or "stories"?

Despite the importance of communicating in a way that connects, guides, and motivates, storytelling is a skill that is rarely mastered or even understood. It is one of those business skills that receives very little (and not enough) attention. Perhaps it's because students are taught to write and speak as young children, so to suggest to business executives or managers that they need to improve their storytelling skills is viewed in some way as demeaning and career limiting. The truth is that communication in all its forms has never been more challenging, or more important.

This issue is so vitally important to leading with vision that understanding and mastering communication—and the art of storytelling in particular—deserves its own special focus. We have already touched on the value of communication when displaying courage, providing clarity, shaping and enhancing the culture, or simply energizing and connecting with people. It is time to focus our understanding now on the art of the storyteller.

So, who are the most effective storytellers—the most successful communicators, motivators, and influencers? What techniques do they use? What aspects about their approach ensure their success? Above all, what does leading with vision actually look and *sound* like? To answer these questions, we decided to start at the top.

THOSE WHO MOVE US

Some of the greatest, most energizing, and best visionary messages of all time are from United States presidents. We remember some of these messages more than others, just as we remember some presidents more than others because some of them—including Lincoln, Kennedy, and Reagan—touched us all. They were masters at painting a picture of where we needed to go and inspiring others to come along.

Ronald Reagan was known for being a master storyteller. His skill was likely developed early on during his time as an actor in Hollywood. After all, acting is storytelling. Reagan was then able to practice and hone his storytelling skill during an eight-year stint as General Electric's pitchman. During this period, about which little is written, Reagan spent twelve weeks a year on tour to GE's 139 facilities. He gave as many as fourteen speeches a day (which makes this a good time to point out that when it comes to storytelling, practice is a very important part of the process).

Reagan developed a style, which he then carried into the presidency. He was funny and warm, often telling stories that felt like a good Western movie. He took listeners' guards down regardless of which side of the political fence they sat on. He moved people and made them want to hear what he had to say. Of course, not everyone wanted to follow him, if for no other reason than his political party, but he did bridge the gap when it came to leading with vision and great storytelling.

Kennedy had the same gift in the 1960s. When we consider that Kennedy was in office for less than three years, it's surprising how much we know about his speeches: "Ask not what your country can do for you—ask what you can do for your country." "*Ich bin ein Berliner.*" "The weapons of war must be abolished before they abolish us." "Yesterday a shaft of light cut into the darkness." We recognize and know these phrases because they were constructed as part of a story and used to punctuate the key messages and move the narrative forward.

Kennedy and Reagan both possessed the skills to deliver carefully crafted words in a way that would influence behavior and opinion.

STORYTELLING AT WORK: WHAT IT MEANS AND WHY IT MATTERS

Storytelling simply means finding a way to connect with an audience by using the powerful and engaging art of communicating through stories. We've all experienced that moment when we hear something that inspires us so much we are instantly fired up and raring to achieve great things. It can be incredibly powerful. Now magnify that throughout an organization and for every day: imagine how much progress that would lead to. All that buzz, excitement, and enthusiasm results from a very special type of person: a storyteller. Specifically, storytellers:

- Put things in motion. They stir things up, agitate the status quo, and create a sense not only of "can do" but also of "want to."
- Excite others through their lively thoughts and behavior. Their energy motivates and inspires people to excel.
- Pull others together and propel them in the same direction.

Storytellers lead inspire, provide clarity, attract, and bind people together.

Storytellers lead, inspire, provide clarity, attract, and bind people together. They animate and provide a compelling tale, of either the past or the future. The work of storytellers sets off a chain reaction that leads to ideas, imagination, commitment, effort, and achievement in many people, who in turn pass this on to other people—and on it goes. This is the power of storytellers.

LEADING PEOPLE THE RIGHT WAY

In today's increasingly complex world, storytellers require something of paramount importance: To get the results they are seeking, they need to lead in the right way. This means leading and working ethically, in a way that is positive and genuine. Why are ethics and integrity so important? Not only do employees and customers benefit from the many policies that are born of ethical considerations, but also integrity has such power because of what it says about the people in charge. Quite simply, it shows that leaders care, and this means people will trust and follow, because they will believe in the place that the leaders are taking them. There is only one way to gain people's trust and inspire them to join in, and that is to be genuine.

DOING THE RIGHT THINGS RIGHT

Storytellers may be energetic, dynamic, and enthusiastic, but how do they enthuse others and generate followership? One way is by infusing integrity into all aspects of the organization, from activities and procedures to achievements and earnings. With today's many media and social media outlets, as well as hackers' ability to break into any system, whatever is really going on in an organization is bound to come out. Without integrity, leaders will not be able to keep followers, because whatever negativity is taking place, it will soon be shared with everyone. Transparency is particularly important to Generation Y, but it has universal appeal.

Storytellers are also tireless. They are constantly honing their stories, devising better ways of saying things, and pushing the boundaries of what is achievable. They are also honest in their storytelling. They show honesty with accuracy, openness, and reliability.

Storytellers must have credibility to be truly heard. People may view leaders as decent, supportive, and fair, but if they feel that the leaders are ordinary, less than impressive, or even incapable, those leaders will not have much influence. Credibility matters.

BALANCING TRANSACTIONAL AND TRANSFORMATIONAL LEADERSHIP THROUGH STORYTELLING

Business today is global. No one can escape it; what happens on the global stage affects us all. This raises an interesting question: are the principal dimensions of successful leadership universally applicable, or do different regions or countries display alternative approaches?

There are distinct differences between transactional leaders, who view relationships as a series of exchanges—"I'll give you this, if you give me that"—and transformational leaders, who seek to change the playing field by moving beyond the usual approach, appreciating the subtleties involved and recognizing the inherent untapped potential to generate new ways of working and new incentives.

TRANSMEDIA STORYTELLERS

We also want to touch on the channels for delivering the message, which are becoming ever more integrated. To gain a better insight into the way that storytelling narratives are being distributed, we had a conversation with Kevin Johnson and Jeff Larsen from a company called In the Telling, who describe themselves as "narrative designers and transmedia storytellers." We had heard through others that they were on the cutting edge of storytelling, and we wanted to understand what *transmedia* means.

Key Questions

Answering the following questions will help you see what is required to be a compelling storyteller and communicator.

1. What makes me want to listen to someone?
2. What makes me feel good about the person I am listening to?
3. What makes me feel negative about the speaker?
4. What do people do that makes me feel comfortable when I am listening to them?
5. What do people do that makes me respect them when I am listening to them?
6. What do people do to lose my respect?
7. What things do people do that distract me when I am listening to them?
8. What mannerisms do I find annoying when listening?
9. What makes me lose interest in a person who is speaking?
10. What subjects arouse strong emotions in me?
11. What topics of discussion do I feel uncomfortable listening to?

12. Do I often think that I already know ahead of time what the speaker is going to say?
13. What do I tend to think about when I am listening to someone?
14. What listening problems do I have?
15. How could I be a better listener?

Kevin described the evolution that is happening with communication: "Film can emotionally connect people to the subject, because it is multisensory. Our brains process images and with music and audio we start emotively connecting to the subject. But it's not just about video. We are in a transitionary period, so people are working with multiple media all the time: we are reading, we are switching into videos, we are switching into music, we are switching into animations."

Jeff used his teenage daughter as a prime example of someone who engages with multiple streams of content across different platforms, often on different devices, almost simultaneously. He noted that this behavior, which is becoming more common, is the driving force behind the transmedia trend.

Transmedia is to digital what illustrations were to the printed book; it's enhancing and enriching the experience. Kevin said, "e-Literate is a great example," and he demonstrated the content on the e-Literate site, which is designed for teachers and professors to "create multiple entry points into a conversation about the issues related to the use of technology in support of education" ("e-literate" 2016).

The site is full of video narrative blogs, but with a difference. Once users click on a video it will play as expected, but if the users prefer, they can read the searchable transcript of the video as it is playing, or they can scan the transcript to move the video to a section they want to listen to. Within the transcript are links to slides and other reference materials that are part of the overall narrative. Users determine their own experience; they can see, hear, read, and interact as they wish. This is transmedia, and it is growing as a medium.

Kevin told us about a transmedia case study for Columbia Business School, which wanted to create a study that was led by a video narrative but was rich in supporting content. The result was called "Operation Tomodachi," a story about Captain Matthew Feely, commanding officer of the U.S. Navy's Fleet Logistics Center, who happened to be the first responder after the Fukushima nuclear reactor disaster in Japan (Ingram and Feely 2016). Not only is it a compelling and fascinating story, but also it is brought to life through interview, documentary footage, photos, and even copies of the emails that were sent back and forth—all available, through the same screen, at the same time. It is a rich transmedia experience that engages and connects with the viewer; it's great storytelling.

In his seminal book *Understanding Media*, Marshall McLuhan (1964) stated that "the medium is the message." We all understand this to a certain extent, but often we can forget it when it is most important. For example, we know that the design, look, feel, and quality of the sales brochure says something about the organization. The medium, in this case a brochure, is in itself a message. But do we apply the same criteria to the staff conference, the monthly newsletter, the intranet? All too often the answer is no, and yet we can see that the medium is just as much a part of the storytelling experience as the message we want to convey.

"The medium is the message."—Marshall McLuhan

When thinking about the best way to tell your story, consider the following:

- How can I tell this story in the most compelling way?
- What's the most appropriate medium for my audience?
- What is the medium that will result in the action/reaction that I want to achieve?
- What medium would add most value to the story?

You as an individual are a communicator—you're the storyteller—but how to distribute the story is up to you, and it often involves decisions around timing, budget, and logistics. However, don't fall into the trap of choosing a method of delivery that is convenient if in fact it does nothing to support your message. Kevin told us that many years ago In the Telling staff members were helping a senior manager to craft a message on improving customer service within her organization. The essence of what she wanted to say was around "the personal touch" and the benefit of building relationships, getting in front of the customers, calling them up, and not just sending them emails. It was a solid message and she was a charismatic leader, but she wanted to record her piece on video and email a link to staff. Ironically, this impersonal approach would have completely undermined her message. When she realized the impact of the medium on the message, she arranged a series of breakfast presentations instead, which went over really well.

SUCCEEDING AS A STORYTELLER

Finally, to be a great storyteller, you have to describe the art of the possible and make people believe they can achieve it. Offering empowerment and shifting mind-set are fundamental aspects of a great story. A key challenge is to promote a positive climate. Negativity can create problems as it often sparks an internal dialogue that distracts the listener. Staying positive can be achieved by emphasizing people's strengths and dealing appropriately with weaknesses by resolving issues. Ensuring that this positive approach permeates the organization will boost morale and energize the people— also, by dealing effectively with any mistakes, leaders will ensure that problems do not become endemic.

A great storyteller has the ability to promote positive connections and communications. By developing close, trusting working relationships, leaders will bring people with them who will, in turn, bring the support of others. Being positive is not a soft option: it motivates and energizes and has a direct impact on the bottom line. By emphasizing people's strengths, leaders ensure that the employees will respond positively, deal with any issues, and improve performance. Blame is counterproductive; problems are best resolved from a positive, "let's make this work" position.

Finally, leaders can empower employees with their message and understand that energy, framing, presence, language, and medium all matter hugely when leading with vision. Encourage a culture of storytelling, not just to communicate vision but also to pass down knowledge, develop skills, and celebrate.

As Roger Schank said in *Tell Me a Story*, "In the end all we have. . .are stories and methods of finding and using those stories" (1995).

TAKEAWAYS FROM CHAPTER 11

- Review some of your recent communications and reflect on whether you are asking the audience to process logic or stories.
- When was the last time you shared a story and what motivated you to share it?
- Leaders who practice their storytelling skills will develop their communication skills—the two go hand in hand.
- The medium is the message. Leaders may want to consider how they will distribute and cascade the message, including what's appropriate for the audience and what's appropriate for the story.

CHAPTER 12

A Blueprint to Creating
a Compelling Vision

As we worked on this book the pieces of the *Leading with Vision* puzzle came together, and our biggest revelation came to us in waves. Over and over again, we were reminded that for all of the talk about cognitive abilities and the more technical characteristics of leadership, when it comes to creating a compelling vision and engaging others around it, the skills required are much softer, much more human. Leaders can get the words exactly right for a compelling vision and still completely miss the human connection. The only way to get people to connect to a vision is to capture their hearts. The emotional connection must be present. When we first started this journey we had a call with a Hollywood playwright, Anthony Grieco (Grieco 2016). Anthony said something that captured our attention: "No one wants to be sold the truth; they want to be sold the romance."

This, of course, does not mean that people want to be lied to. Instead, it means that people crave more than truth, facts, and intellectual understanding. Human beings are emotional creatures, and if employees are going to enthusiastically help deliver a vision, they need to be emotionally connected.

The model for *Leading with Vision* is called "LIFT6: Leadership to Inspire Future Talent," because creating a compelling vision is all about inspiring your talent and helping them to focus on your organization's future.

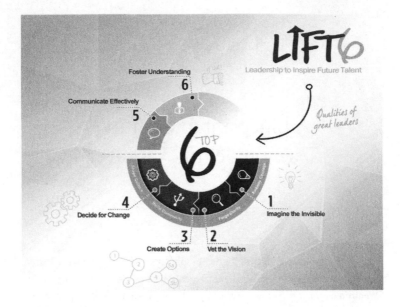

All leaders can lead with vision if they are willing to do what it takes. There are the six pieces to the puzzle:

1. Imagine the invisible.
2. Vet the vision.
3. Create options.
4. Decide for change.
5. Communicate Effectively
6. Foster understanding.

Let's walk through it.

1. IMAGINE THE INVISIBLE

Now, let's think about this for a moment. When we talk about the invisible, what are we really talking about? The invisible isn't a prediction of the future; it is more a seed of an idea that has yet to sprout. It is without boundaries. It isn't held back by the past. It could change the world. It is not yet tangible or visual; it is invisible.

"Vision is the art of seeing the invisible."

—Jonathan Swift

Now imagine how difficult it is to create that seed, and even more, how difficult it is to share and communicate that seed. Leaders not only need to see and live the invisible, but also they need to communicate the invisible, share the invisible, and promote the invisible to truly inspire others around the vision.

Abraham Lincoln was an American politician and lawyer who served as the sixteenth president of the United States. He had a compelling vision—the abolishment of slavery—and he rallied a country to help achieve it. In a country where states were still passing laws restricting the rights of black citizens, the idea of abolishing slavery was an invisible vision. At the Ford Museum in Washington, D.C., there are books about his legacy stacked four stories high, and his legacy comes down to his vision for two things: pass the Thirteenth Amendment to abolish slavery and win America's Civil War, thus preserving the union and strengthening the federal government. He did so in the face of great personal adversity and with great opposition to his leadership. Lincoln imagined victory and the abolition of slavery and then he helped others imagine it too. Imagining the invisible and then sharing it isn't always easy, but it is worth it.

2. VET THE VISION

As we discussed in chapter 9, vetting the vision is one of the best ways to get buy-in throughout the organization. In fact, not taking the time to get buy-in is a recipe for disaster. According to Merriam-Webster.com, to vet something is "to check (something) carefully to make sure it is acceptable" ("Vet" n.d.). Vetting your vision can be done in any number of unique and specific ways that best fit your organization. One of our favorite ways involves putting out a vision that is not quite fully formed, such as in Bruce A. Strong's work with Red Hat Corporation described in chapter 9, and then creating those powerful strategic conversations throughout the organization. No matter how leaders choose to vet the vision, the goal is to get others involved: working on it, thinking about it, improving it, and sharing it.

At Executive Development Associates, we have a process for the custom design of leadership programs, and it involves an off-site retreat for the actual design workshop. We always ask organizations to include those noisy influencers in the organization regardless of where they lie in the hierarchy, because when we leave the design process, we want to make sure that the "noise" is in our favor. The vision has to mean something to the people who are going to help achieve it, and the only way that will happen is if it ignites their passions.

Think back to our story about Patagonia, the designer of outdoor sports clothing, where employees take the stairs two at a time on the way to work. People who work at Patagonia buy into the vision of creating great products that cause minimal damage to the environment at a fundamental and personal level. Most are hikers, surfers, mountain climbers, and skiers themselves, and they know that what is being made matters.

3. CREATE OPTIONS

In the finance world, an option is "a financial derivative that represents a contract sold by one party (the option writer) to another party (the option holder). The contract offers the buyer the right, but not the obligation, to buy (call) or sell (put) a security or other financial asset at an agreed-upon price (the strike price) during a certain period of time or on a specific date (exercise date)" ("Option" n.d). Similarly, as a method to address the ever-shifting uncertainty of today's business environment, organizations can mitigate their risk by creating options, thus giving them the right, but not the obligation, to pursue designated paths. In the past, organizations set the vision, created a strategy, and pursued it aggressively.

In our *Trends* research, 466 companies identified cognitive readiness as one of the key skills required of leaders in medium and large companies today. Cognitive readiness is the mental, emotional, and interpersonal preparedness for uncertainty and risk. Cognitive readiness is an umbrella term for higher-order thinking skills. Two of these skills that are needed to create options for a compelling vision and long-term organizational success are adaptability and agility.

> *Cognitive readiness is an umbrella term for higher-order thinking skills.*

- Adaptability means to be "able to change or be changed in order to fit or work better in some situation or for some purpose" ("Adaptability" n.d.).
- Agility is the ability to be "able to move quickly and easily; quick, smart, and clever" ("Agility" n.d.).

When the winds shift or a storm arises, each organization had better be ready to shift as well. Having multiple options well thought out and built into the plan will make this easier for leaders, because when the winds shift, there often isn't time to go back to the drawing board. Decisions have to be made quickly and correctly.

4. DECIDE FOR CHANGE

Albert Einstein said the definition of insanity is "doing the same thing over and over again and expecting different results." Having a compelling vision of a positive future state is going to require changes in the shared picture of the future, in thinking, and in behavior. Deciding for change means stepping up and putting action to the vision. It's time to make decisions, establish plans, and set goals.

We have built a blueprint to guide our clients during our vision workshops; we also use it with our own companies when we work on vision and strategy. You can download it for free from our website *(www .leadingwith.vision)*.

The blueprint is based on the concept of appreciative inquiry (AI), a model that "seeks to engage stakeholders in self-determined change." The belief with AI is that leaders have the answers; they just need to ask the right questions. Here is the blueprint:

Visionary Future State:

Mentally put yourself in the future, typically three to five years out. Imagine where your organization could be, where it should be. Describe what it will look like when this is accomplished. Use descriptive words so that you and others can envision what it will look like and be like. Try to be as specific and clear as possible.

Current State

What does it look like today? What is currently happening? What are the problems? What is the impact of the current situation?

Key Stakeholders

Who will be impacted if the future outcome comes true? Who are the people who will need to be engaged for the vision to become reality?

Barriers or Challenges

What are the obstacles that will have to be overcome in order to be successful?

Enhancers and Support

List anything that will help move the organization in the right direction. People, finances, infrastructure.

Goals and Action Steps

List your goals. State action steps that will need to be taken in order to get from the current state to the future state.

1. Goal

- Action
- Action
- Action
- Action

2. Goal

- Action
- Action
- Action
- Action

3. Goal

- Action
- Action
- Action
- Action

4. Goal

- Action
- Action
- Action
- Action

5. Goal

- Action
- Action
- Action
- Action

Measure Success

What can be measured to track the progress?

5. COMMUNICATE EFFECTIVELY

Once you have made the necessary decisions to advance the vision, concentrating on communication and cascading the message are next. When it is time for leaders to communicate where they want to go, they really can't do too much, but they can do it poorly. Remember everything that we have said about the need for stories and storytelling. Once leaders have the story structured, then they should shout it from the mountain and whisper it through the trees. Communicating the compelling vision must become a core part of the discussions throughout the organization.

Communicating the compelling vision should be a core part of the discussions throughout the organization.

CEOs and their teams must ensure that board members also clearly understand and are in agreement with where the organization intends to go. The senior team needs to be talking about it both in daily conversations and in regular—ideally monthly—meetings designed to pull the vision forward. Down through the organization, in every department, employees need to be talking about how to work the plan and bring the vision to pass.

For example, it's easy to imagine that the employees of Patagonia are continuously having conversations about how they build great products that allow people to experience the outdoors in unique ways while having as little negative impact as possible on the environment. Similarly, Jimbo's didn't just make one statement about GMO; it's part of every conversation they have with employees, suppliers, and customers. If the people in a company who are closest to the customer are not continuously thinking about the vision and how to get there, then the leader hasn't reached them yet, which leads us to our final puzzle piece.

6. FOSTER UNDERSTANDING

Reaching employees at the day-to-day work level—where they are thinking about and actually trying to achieve the vision—means that leaders foster understanding for employees about their role. There is an old story about a janitor at the National Aeronautics and Space Administration (NASA) that makes the point really well.

> During a visit to the NASA space center in 1962, President John F. Kennedy noticed a janitor carrying a broom. He interrupted his tour, walked over to the man, and said, "Hi, I'm Jack Kennedy. What are you doing?"
>
> "Well, Mr. President," the janitor responded, "I'm helping put a man on the moon" (Nemo 2014).

We've seen successful leaders use this approach throughout the book as well. For example, nurses at St. Luke's need to understand how their role in each patient interaction contributes to the *My St. Luke's* identity. At Bumble Bee, the people on the line packing cans of tuna need to understand how their job is impacting the organization's ability to be the leading brand in the industry, and they need to recognize that the brand will mean health, sustainability, and conservation to the customer. It has to get real and personal.

IMPLEMENTING THE FUNDAMENTALS

Leaders also need to embody courage, forge clarity, build community, and shape the culture. Let's look at each practice in turn.

Embody Courage

What is it about human nature that causes people to like leaders with courage? We all love the bold, the brave, and the audacious. We all want to try new things, go to new places, and build new entities. Consequently, we all melt when leaders have the courage to get real and share their personal pain, shame, and struggles. Courage is exciting and compelling. Playing it safe may be okay and even required for accountants and lawyers, but for those who want to lead an organization with a compelling vision, courage has to be the leading ingredient.

Another, less-discussed element of courage is the courage for leaders to become very aware of their own ability to impact the culture. This includes taking an objective look at their position, level of influence, and personal energy for achieving the vision. After all, if leaders can't get passionate about it, then it's impossible to expect others to get there.

Every leader has strengths and weaknesses. This is a good time to evaluate yours when it comes to reaching the vision and then make plans to build on your strengths and overcome, minimize, or get help for your weaknesses.

Strengths are the best place to start. Look for the best potential home-run hits: the two or three things that you do very well—maybe exceptionally well—where it's a knock-it-out-of-the-park home-run, even if it only happens once or twice a year.

While dwelling on them is not helpful, you can still recognize and work to minimize your weaknesses. These are the areas that drag you down. If you're going to be remembered for one or two home-run hits a year, you are probably also going to be remembered for one or two major screwups each year. Weaknesses are typically where we initiate our major screwups. For me personally, my weakness is a lack of patience. When I have a problem, it's usually because I didn't have the patience to get more data or ask for more feedback or let things settle awhile before taking action. For Simon, it's enjoying the detail for too long and not lifting his head up to see the bigger picture sooner. For John, it's trying to do too many things at once; if you're spinning plates, the chances are high that one will fall eventually.

We all have them. What are yours? Take a moment to think about it and write them down.

Strengths for Leading with Vision

_____

_____

_____

_____

Weaknesses for Leading with Vision

_____

_____

_____

_____

Forge Clarity

Clarity is a beautiful word. Close your eyes for a minute. Imagine some-one taking a spoon and tapping a crystal glass. Can you hear the note that it makes? It's pure. It's clear. It's beautiful. That's clarity. When we get clarity right, the note—in this case the compelling vision—travels down through the organization with an ease that comes only from being extremely clear. Remember that the emerging generation sees a company not as a spreadsheet but as a story, and they are characters in the story. If the story isn't clear and clearly communicated, their characters in the story will not be clearly defined, and they will not contribute at the highest possible level.

Build Connectivity

The generation that will rule the world in the very near future is all about community and connectedness. For employees to be engaged around a compelling vision, there must be a sense of "we are in this together." The workforce members of Generation Y don't want to do a solo performance. They want to work with their friends. They even move around in pods. In fact, if you want to keep your Generation Y employees, hire their friends, and then ensure that the whole pack understands their part in the story.

Shape Culture

Vision and strategy are just words until they are embedded into culture. Remember that culture, at its core, is the way that your employees see and experience how things get done. Culture exists in a business, community, city, or county, but just because it exists doesn't mean it can't be shaped. Once a compelling vision is set, the senior leaders must spend time thinking about what behaviors and ways of doing things need to be established in the organization in order to achieve the vision. The stronger the culture, the better. For example, Hilti has a strong and productive culture, and to ensure that it stays that way, they require all 22,000 employees to go through a two-day culture workshop every two years.

Seeing different cultures in action is fascinating. In some companies, the employees are out the door trying to deliver before the instructions have been completely explained, while in other companies, the employees spend a significant amount of time ensuring that each instruction is fully understood. In some cultures, decisions require a committee, while in other cultures, there isn't a committee in sight. Some cultures build on idea after idea while others take one idea and run it to its full completion. As leaders move their organization forward, they must intentionally shape, model, and guide the culture in the direction that will help the company achieve its vision.

GET SOME SUPPORT

Listen, we all need a little help from our friends now and then, and this is the time to ask for it. After all, we're talking about community and connectedness, right? Here are some ways in which you can get help to achieve a compelling vision and engage others around it.

Team coaching. Team coaching is a great way to support and challenge each other as you go through the vision work processes. Team coaching typically involves a coach working with an entire team or teams to move things forward. The team coach will help the team work through difficult issues, debate ideas, and build positive and encouraging plans to go forward.

Executive coaching. Individual coaching is another way to help maintain energy and focus. Typically, executive coaching is a one-on-one experience lasting three to six months to identify and address strengths and weaknesses.

Personal support. Of course, work colleagues are not by any means the only way to get support for your work adventures. It's also possible to involve your family, friends, spouse, or partner as you think through how to lead the organization to a compelling vision and also about your own leadership steps and missteps. Leading with vision is a very human endeavor, and it's important to tap all of your human support systems in order to get there.

TAKEAWAYS FROM CHAPTER 12

- Work through the LIFT6 Model: *Leadership to Inspire Future Talent*:
    - Imagine the invisible
    - Vet the vision
    - Create options
    - Decide for change
    - Communicate effectively
    - Foster understanding
- Write a sentence to state how you will address the following:
    - Embody courage.
    - Forge clarity.
    - Build community.
    - Shape culture.
- Make a note of your support network and who you can use to help develop areas where you need to improve.

CHAPTER 13

Conclusion

W E STARTED ON THIS JOURNEY because the research we had seen was telling us that there is a gap between what we need from our leaders and what they are delivering. There are competing priorities when it comes to leadership development, and too many organizations are focusing on short-term financial performance and ignoring the greater threats that are looming. Advances in technology, globalization, and changing consumer behavior are familiar challenges that leaders continue to face on a daily basis. But the new threat comes from within, in the form of a generation of workers who have very different expectations from previous generations. Instead of being beaten into shape by corporate behavior, the millennials (Generation Y) are causing some of the biggest businesses in the world to rethink how they engage with the people they want to be the future of their organizations. Specifically, the fact that this generation is as disruptive to organizational culture as technology has been is something that leaders need to understand—and understand quickly.

According to the research that started us on this journey, we need compelling visions and visionary leaders. Visionary leaders can build and create from nothing. When there is no visible path ahead, they see one; they make one. Visionary leaders take their employees to new places, and that's what they need; that's what they demand. Perhaps the reason visionary leadership is so needed now is because our world is changing, and it's uncomfortable. Vaclav Havel (1994), the first president of the Czech Republic, said once, "I think there are good reasons for suggesting that the modern age has ended. Today, many things indicate that we are going through a transitional period, when it seems that something is on the way out and something else is painfully being born. It is as if something were crumbling, decaying, and exhausting itself, while something else, still indistinct, were arising from the rubble." And that is the VUCA (volatile, uncertain, complex, and ambiguous) environment that people talk about today, more than twenty years after Havel's speech. Visionary leaders lead through it. They help us get to new, unexplored places.

It is worth understanding what leading with vision involves—and what it does not. The components of leading with vision are not ingenuity, originality, sheer intellect, or brilliance, as valuable as these may be. Instead, leading with vision means looking ahead to what could be and what should be, and then finding a way to *connect* powerfully with the people who can get you there. This is done by having the *courage* to be both bold and vulnerable. People often confuse courage and boldness (vital for leading with vision) with originality and exceptionality (useful, but certainly not essential). Consider this particularly effective vision:

> We choose to go to the moon in this decade and do the other things—not because they are easy, but because they are hard. Because that goal will serve to organize and measure the best of our abilities and skills, because that challenge is one that we are willing to accept, one we are unwilling to postpone, and one which we intend to win. (*President John F. Kennedy*)

Essentially, President Kennedy was suggesting that having failed to put the first man into Earth's orbit, America's space agency should instead go to the moon. Bold and courageous? Certainly. Clear and unequivocal? Absolutely. Exciting and inspiring in a way that resonated and connected with people? Of course—the results prove this, together with the fact that people still remember those powerful words. But *exceptional*, really? A space agency going to the moon in the early days of spaceflight was, frankly, to be expected. What elevates Kennedy's vision is not intellect or even originality: it is everything else.

Leading with vision means providing *clarity* about the vision—what it will mean and what it can achieve. Clarity awakens our senses and has the ability to surprise and touch us in unexpected ways. Remember how the world tuned in when the unknown and slightly sassy singer named Susan Boyle stepped onto center stage for the television show *Britain's Got Talent*? Susan Boyle walked out to face the judges and audience with her vision in mind, which she described to Simon Cowell, one of the judges, as "to be a professional singer." The audience reacted by raising their eyebrows, sneering, and mumbling to each other.

Piers Morgan, another judge, asked, "What are you going sing?"

Boyle replied, "'I Dreamed a Dream,' from the musical *Les Misérables*" (Boyle 2009). The panel of judges looked skeptical, and as the cameras cut away to the audience, it was clear that they too couldn't equate the woman standing on stage with an iconic song from a classic musical. And then she began to sing. The judges' wry smiles shifted into dropped jaws and their eyes widened; the crowd, who only seconds before had dismissed her, were now whooping, clapping, and standing on their feet. After just thirty seconds, she won over the whole auditorium as well as the millions of viewers who were watching at home. People watching were a little shocked, moved, and awakened. Her song touched the world and touched our hearts. Her tone was so crystal clear, her message so moving. As of today, the YouTube video of Susan's first song on the show has been viewed 198,031,888 times. That's what clarity does. It cuts through chaos and focuses our senses. It cuts through the fog.

In our organizations, we see the need for clarity every day. We usually call our fog things like *economic turmoil, disruptive ideas, demographic shift*, or *corporate bureaucracy*. According to Gary Hamel and Michele Zanini, "More people are working in big, bureaucratic organizations than ever before. Yet there's compelling evidence that bureaucracy creates a significant drag on productivity and organizational resilience and innovation. By our reckoning, the cost of excess bureaucracy in the U.S. economy amounts to more than $3 trillion in lost economic output, or about 17 percent of GDP" (2016). With numbers like these, it's worth it to get clarity right.

Sense of community has been a major factor in the stories that we have heard, which might be surprising given that we are talking about businesses. But the world has changed, and where visionary leadership used to be all jargon, models, and acronyms, that method of leading isn't going to work anymore. The models don't create points of differentiation or competitive advantage now—if they ever did. Instead, people are the differentiators, and, as such, leaders must view them in a new light. Leaders can bring employees along by engaging with them and connecting with them. Leaders need to remember that they are only a leader if others follow.

Leaders who ensure that the employees are an essential part of creating, shaping, or finishing the vision do so because other perspectives and experiences enrich the vision and make it better. Even more than that, leaders will be able to engage others around a compelling vision if they are willing to connect with their employees on a much more personal level, intentionally creating a community. Examples we've shown here have included Hilti's focus on using customer service representatives who live in the neighborhoods where they provide service, and OluKai's family meal gatherings with staff. The employees (and friends) of both organizations responded with a wholeheartedness not seen in many companies, because humans like to feel connected. They want to do life together, even if it gets a little messy from time to time. Humans enjoy reaching for something collectively, caring about what happens to each other, eating, laughing, working, and struggling together.

Another key component that we explored in this book is culture, the heavyweight component of leading with vision. Turning a workforce into a community of highly engaged professionals who are willing to spend their time and energy to achieve a compelling vision means that the highest-level leaders must intentionally shape the *culture* into one of excitement, inspiration, and relevant, purposeful action. The intentionality of driving culture is central. Great visions rely on a positive culture with a sense of urgency. Or, put another way, a weak or negative culture will frustrate and continually challenge progress toward the vision, while a positive culture with a sense of urgency will facilitate it.

In fact, when it comes to the effect of culture on the realization of a vision, it either helps or hinders—there is no middle ground. The stronger the culture is, the better the results are. As we saw with the companies featured throughout the book, building the right culture to achieve the vision and engaging a workforce around it means setting up systems, creating and delivering training, and ensuring that executives are present and are modeling behavior from as high up as the members of the board. It means leading from the top to the bottom. It requires an investment of commitment, time, and money.

The personal commitment of the leader is the final piece of the *Leading with Vision* puzzle. Unless leaders are willing to imagine the future, learn to communicate powerfully, and work on their own development, leading with vision isn't possible. All leaders who want to lead with vision must give of themselves in a way that feels—and actually is—risky.

Leading with vision demands a giving of self: a willingness to admit weaknesses and a willingness to change and grow. Although it's challenging, it's worth it. Leaders who give of themselves get it all back, because they experience an opportunity to touch others in a very personal and positive sense. Above all else, leading with vision is a gratifying way to reach others: to guide them, to help them at work and, sometimes, even at home—ultimately affecting people's lives for the positive.

References

CHAPTER 1

1. Hagemann, Bonnie, Heather Ishikawa, Sattar Bawany, Louise Korver, and Steve Terrell, eds. *Trends in Executive Development 2016: A Benchmark Report*. Executive Development Associates, February 22, 2016. *https://executivedevelopment.com/online-solutions/product/2016-trends-in-executive-development/*.

2. McLeod, Saul. "Maslow's Hierarchy of Needs." *Simply Psychology*. 2013. Accessed November 14, 2016. *www.simplypsychology.org/maslow.html*.

CHAPTER 2

1. Chouinard, Yvon. *Let My People Go Surfing: The Education of a Reluctant Businessman*. New York: Penguin Press, 2005.

2. Delaney, Pete. Interview by Bonnie Hagemann. August 1, 2016.

3. Fallon Taylor, Nicole. "What Is a Mission Statement?" *Business News Daily*, January 7, 2015. *www.businessnewsdaily.com/3783-mission-statement.html*.

4. LeVan, AJ, MAPP. "Seeing Is Believing: The Power of Visualization." *Psychology Today*, December 3, 2009. *www.psychologytoday.com/blog/flourish/200912/seeing-is-believing-the-power-visualization*.

5. Mathieu, John E., and Dennis M. Zajac. "A Review and Meta-analysis of the Antecedents, Correlates, and Consequences of Organizational Commitment." *Psychological Bulletin* 108, no. 2 (1990): 171–94, doi:10.1037/0033-2909.108.2.171.

6. Mowday, Richard T., Lyman W. Porter, and Richard M. Steers. *Employee-organization Linkages: The Psychology of Commitment, Absenteeism, and Turnover*. New York: Academic Press, 1982.

7. Neason, Matt. "The Power of Visualization." *Sport Psychology Today*, August 8, 2012. *www.sportpsychologytoday.com/sport-psychology-for-coaches/the-power-of-visualization/*.

8. Pinder, Craig C. *Work Motivation in Organizational Behavior*. Upper Saddle River, NJ: Prentice Hall, 2008.

9. Pritchard, Robert D., and Stephanie C. Payne. "Performance Management Practices and Motivation." In *The New Workplace: A Guide to the Human Impact of Modern Working Practices*, edited by D. Holman, T. D. Wall, C. W. Clegg, P. Sparrow, and A. Howard. Chichester, U.K.: John Wiley & Sons, Ltd, 2002. doi: 10.1002/9780470713365.ch12.

CHAPTER 3

1. Anderson, Rick. Interview by Bonnie Hagemann. August 1, 2016.

2. Dubuque, Susan. Interview by Bonnie Hagemann. August 1, 2016.

3. LeVan, AJ, "Seeing Is Believing: The Power of Visualization." *Psychology Today*, December 3, 2009. *www.psychologytoday.com/blog/flourish/200912/seeing-is-believing-the-power-visualization*.

4. Lischewski, Chris. Interview by Simon Vetter. August 12, 2015.

5. Neason, Matt. "The Power of Visualization." *Sport Psychology Today*, August 8, 2012. *www.sportpsychologytoday.com/sport-psychology-for-coaches/the-power-of-visualization/*.

CHAPTER 4

1. Aristotle, W. D. Ross, and Lesley Brown. *Nicomachean Ethics*. Oxford: Oxford University Press, 2009.

2. Bina, Shideh Sedgh. "Culture Eats Everything for Breakfast, Lunch and Dinner." *Insigniam Quarterly* 4, no. 3 (Summer 2016): 1.

3. Braun, Frank, and Michael Avital. "Good Project Management Practices Drive More than Project Success: Learning, Knowledge Sharing and Job Satisfaction in IT Project Teams." *Proceedings of the 13th Americas Conference on Information Systems at Colorado* (August 9–12, 2007) 1–11. *http://toc.proceedings.com/01774webtoc.pdf.*

4. "Courage." *Merriam-Webster.com.* Merriam-Webster, n.d. Web. 11 August 2016.

5. "Generation Y: Entrepreneur." *Journal of Property Management 77,* no. 3 (May/June 2012). *www.questia.com/magazine/1P3-2666488501/generation-y-entrepreneur.*

6. Hagemann, Bonnie, Heather Ishikawa, Sattar Bawany, Louise Korver, and Steve Terrell, eds. *Trends in Executive Development 2016: A Benchmark Report.* Executive Development Associates. February 22, 2016. *https://executivedevelopment.com/online-solutions/product/2016-trends-in-executive-development/.*

7. Hennessey, J. T. "'Reinventing' Government: Does Leadership Make the Difference?" *Public Administration Review 58,* no. 6 (1998): 522–32.

8. Howell, Elizabeth. "Virgin Galactic Will Recover from Tragic Crash, Richard Branson Says." Space.com, January 3, 2015. *www.space.com/28154-virgin-galactic-spaceshiptwo-crash-recovery.html.*

9. Kouzes, James M., and Barry Z. Posner. *The Leadership Challenge: How to Make Extraordinary Things Happen in Organizations.* San Francisco: Jossey-Bass, 2012.

10. "KPMG Revolutionises Its Approach to Graduate Recruitment." *Smart Thinking: News* (July 27, 2016). *www.kpmgcareers.co.uk/smart-thinking/news/articles/kpmg-launch-pad.*

11. Martin, Jason. "'That's the Way We Do Things Around Here': An Overview of Organizational Culture." *Electronic Journal of Academic and Special Librarianship 7,* no. 1 (Spring 2006). *http://southernlibrarianship.icaap.org/content/v07n01/martin_m01.htm.*

12. "Millennials at Work: Reshaping the Workplace." 2011. *www.pwc.com/gx/en/managing-tomorrows-people/future-of-work/assets/reshaping-the-workplace.pdf.*

13. Mowday, Richard T., Richard M. Steers, and Lyman W. Porter. "The Measurement of Organizational Commitment." *Journal of Vocational Behavior* 14 (1979): 224–47.

14. Ridderstråle, Jonas, and Kjell A. Nordström. *Karaoke Capitalism: Management for Mankind.* Harlow: Financial Times Prentice Hall, 2004.

15. Schein, Edgar H. *Organizational Culture and Leadership.* San Francisco: Jossey-Bass, 1992.

16. Simons, Tony, Ray Friedman, Leigh Anne Liu, and Judi McLean Parks. "Racial Differences in Sensitivity to Behavioral Integrity: Attitudinal Consequences, In-Group Effects, and 'Trickle Down' among Black and Non-Black Employees." *Journal of Applied Psychology* 92, no. 3 (2007): 650–65.

17. Weingart, Laurie R., and Elizabeth Weldon. "Processes that Mediate the Relationship between a Group Goal and Group Member Performance." *Human Performance* 4 (1991): 33–54, doi:10.1207/s15327043hup0401_2.

CHAPTER 5

1. American Customer Satisfaction Survey. "ACSI 2015 Year in Review: Slumping Customer Satisfaction across Much of the U.S. Economy." News release, December 29, 2015. *www.theacsi.org/news-and-resources/press-releases/press-2015/press-release-acsi-year-in-review-2015.*

2. Bastean, Todd. Interview by Bonnie Hagemann. August 1, 2016.

3. Brown, Brené. *Daring Greatly: How the Courage to Be Vulnerable Transforms the Way We Live, Love, Parent, and Lead.* New York: Gotham Books, 2012.

4. Burns, Megan, Harley Manning, Carla O'Connor, and Colin Camp-bell. "The Customer Experience Index, 2014." Forrester.com, January 24, 2014. *www.forrester.com/report/The Customer Experience Index 2014/-/E-RES109081*.

5. "French Proverbs Dictionary | Language Realm." Accessed November 27, 2016. *www.languagerealm.com/french/frenchproverbs_c.php&p= DevEx,5077.1*.

6. Grenacher, Michael. Interview by Simon Vetter. August 1, 2015.

7. "The Jimbo's Ethos: Jimbo's...Naturally! Bill of Rights." *http://jimbos .com/the-jimbos-difference/the-jimbos-ethos/*.

8. "Jimbo's...Naturally! San Diego, CA." *http://oca-orca.org/store/ jimbos-naturally-carlsbad-ca/*.

9. Mercola, J. "Dr Mercola interviews Jim 'Jimbo' Someck," September 2012, *www.youtube.com/watch?v=nSnYuvOoCV8*.

10. 'Jimbo's...Naturally! San Diego, CA' (company profile and interview) Organic Retail and Consumer Alliance, 2013, *http://oca-orca.org/ store/jimbos-naturally-carlsbad-ca/*.

11. "Verint-Commissioned Research Reveals Superior Customer Service Beats Price in Asia Pacific Markets." Verint.com, August 27, 2013. *www.verint.com/news-events/press-releases/2013-pr-archives/08-27 -13*.

CHAPTER 6

1. Berg, Ulf. Interview by Simon Vetter. August 1, 2015.

2. Groysberg, Boris, and Michael Slind. "The Silent Killer of Big Com-panies." *Harvard Business Review,* October 25, 2012. *https://hbr.org/ 2012/10/the-silent-killer-of-big-companies*.

3. Huy, Quy. "Who Killed Nokia? Nokia Did." *INSEAD Knowledge,* Sep-tember 22, 2016. *http://knowledge.insead.edu/strategy/who-killed -nokia-nokia-did-4268*.

4. Lofaso, Chris. Interview by Simon Vetter. August 1, 2015.

5. Surowiecki, James. "Where Nokia Went Wrong." *New Yorker,* September 3, 2013. *www.newyorker.com/business/currency/where-nokia-went -wrong.*

6. Troianovski, Anton, and Sven Grundberg. "Nokia's Bad Call on Smartphones." *Wall Street Journal,* July 18, 2012. *www.wsj.com/ articles/SB10001424052702304388004577531002591315494.*

CHAPTER 7

1. Harris, Jim. Interview by Simon Vetter. June 15, 2016.

2. "History, Reliability & Validity of the FIRO-B® Instrument." *CPP— The People Development People. www.cpp.com/Products/firo-b/firob_ info.aspx.*

3. Proodian, Cheryl. Interview by Simon Vetter. June 16, 2016.

4. Schnell, Eugene R., and Allen L. Hammer. *Introduction to the FIRO-B Instrument in Organizations.* Mountain View, CA: CPP, 2004.

CHAPTER 8

1. Bina, Shideh Sedgh. "Culture Eats Everything for Breakfast, Lunch and Dinner." *Insigniam Quarterly* 4, no. 3 (Summer 2016): 1.

2. "Company History—Hilti Corporation." Hilti.com. Accessed November 27, 2016. *www.hilti.com/company-history.*

3. Hindle, Tim. "Global Player from a Very Small Country: The Case of Hilti." *Korn Ferry,* October 10, 2011. *www.kornferry.com/institute/ 28-global-player-from-a-very-small-country-the-case-of-hilti.*

4. "Home—Hilti Corporation." *Hilti.com. https://hilti.com/.*

5. Slaaen, Eivind. Interview by Simon Vetter. September 1, 2016.

6. "Vision and Values—Hilti Corporation." Hilti.com. www.hilti.com/vision-and-values.

CHAPTER 9

1. "About the New York Public Library." The New York Public Library. Accessed November 27, 2016. *www.nypl.org/help/about-nypl.*

2. "Achiever's Intelligence: Insight into Today's Workforce." 2012. *https://fortunedotcom.files.wordpress.com/2012/06/wp_achieversintelligence .pdf.*

3. Hansen, Morten. Collaboration: How Leaders Avoid the Traps, Create Unity, and Reap Big Results. Boston: Harvard Business School Press, 2009.

4. Isern, Joseph, and Caroline Pung. "Organizing for Successful Change Management: A McKinsey Global Survey." *McKinsey Quarterly,* June 2006.

5. Keller, Scott, Mary Meaney, and Caroline Pung. "What Successful Transformations Share: McKinsey Global Survey Results." McKinsey & Company, 2010. *www.mckinsey.com/business-functions/organization/our-insights/what-successful-transformations-share-mckinsey -global-survey-results.*

6. Spender, J.-C., and Bruce A. Strong. *Strategic Conversations: Creating and Directing the Entrepreneurial Workforce.* Cambridge: Cambridge University Press, 2014.

7. Welch, J., and Byrne, J. *Straight from the Gut.* New York: Warner Business Books, 2001.

8. YouTube. Accessed November 27, 2016. *www.youtube.com/watch?v=hq2CnccWdPs.*

9. Zillman, Claire. "With Co-CEOs, Companies Flirt with Disaster." *Fortune,* September 20, 2014. *www.fortune.com/2014/09/20/oracle -two-ceos-disaster/.*

CHAPTER 10

1. *Alien.* S.l. : Twentieth Century Fox, 2004.

2. "Anecdote." *Merriam-Webster.com.* Merriam-Webster, n.d. Web. August 11, 2016.

3. "Aphorism." *Merriam-Webster.com.* Merriam-Webster, n.d. Web. August 11, 2016.

4. Aristotle and D. W. Lucas. *The Poetics.* Oxford: Clarendon Press, 1968.

5. Bagozzi, Richard P., Mahesh Gopinath, and Prashanth U. Nyer. "The Role of Emotions in Marketing." *Journal of the Academy of Marketing Science* 27, no. 2 (1999): 184–206, doi:10.1177/0092070399272005.

6. Beilenson, Peter, Harry Behn, and Jeff Hill. *Haiku Harvest: Japanese Haiku, Series IV.* Mount Vernon, NY: Peter Pauper, 1962.

7. Chakrabarty, Prosanta. "Clues to Prehistoric Times, Found in Blind Cavefish." TED.com, filmed February 2016. *www.ted.com/talks/ prosanta_chakrabarty_clues_to_prehistoric_times_found_in_blind_ cavefish.*

8. "Contradiction." Merriam-Webster.com. Merriam-Webster, n.d. Web. August 11, 2016.

9. *"Creator of TED Conference: 'I Hate Being Spoken To.'"* Video produced by Leah Binkovitz and Ryan R. Reed. Smithsonian.com, 2012. *www .smithsonianmag.com/videos/category/innovation/creator-of-ted -conference-i-hate-being-spo/.*

10. *Dead Poets Society.* United States: Buena Vista Pictures Distribution, 1989.

11. Hubbard, Elbert. *Loyalty in Business: And One and Twenty Other Good Things.* East Aurora, NY: Printed by the Roycrofters, 1921.

12. Lerner, Jennifer, Ye Li, Piercarlo Valdesolo, and Karim Kassam. "Emotion and Decision Making." *Annual Review of Psychology* 66 (January 2015): 799–823.

13. Zetlin, Minda. "The 9 Worst Mission Statements of All Time." Inc. com, 2013. *www.inc.com/minda-zetlin/9-worst-mission-statements-all -time.html*.

CHAPTER 11

1. "E-Literate." E-Literate. Accessed November 27, 2016. *http://mfeldstein .com/*.

2. "Email Statistics Report, 2015–2019." Radicati Group Inc. RSS, March 2015. *www.radicati.com/*.

3. Grieco, Anthony. Interview by Bonnie Hagemann and Simon Vetter. January 2016.

4. Ingram, Paul, and Captain Matthew S. Feely. "Operation Tomodachi." Columbia CaseWorks, Columbia Business School, 2013. *www8.gsb .columbia.edu/caseworks/node/436*.

5. Johnson, Kevin, and Larsen, Jeff. Interview by John Maketa. July 2016.

6. McLuhan, Marshall. *Understanding Media: The Extensions of Man.* The MIT Press, 1964.

7. Plato. *Phaedrus.* Oxford World's Classics, 2009.

8. Schank, Roger C. *Tell Me a Story: Narrative and Intelligence.* Evanston, IL: Northwestern University Press, 1995.

9. Weisberg, Jacob. "The Road to Reagandom." *slate*, 2016. *www .slate.com/articles/news_and_politics/politics/2016/01/ronald_reagan _s_conservative_conversion_as_spokesman_for_general_electric .html*.

CHAPTER 12

1. "Adaptable." Merriam-Webster.com. Accessed September 4, 2016. *www.merriam-webster.com/dictionary/adaptable*.

2. "Agility." Merriam-Webster.com. Accessed September 4, 2016. *https:// www.merriam-webster.com/dictionary/agility*.

3. Nemo, John. "What a NASA Janitor Can Teach Us about Living a Bigger Life." *Business Journals*, 2014. *www.bizjournals.com/bizjournals/ how-to/growth-strategies/2014/12/what-a-nasa-janitor-can-teach-us .html.*

4. "Option." Investopedia. 2016. Accessed September 04, 2016. *http:// www.investopedia.com/terms/o/option.asp.*

5. "Vet." Merriam-Webster.com. Accessed September 4, 2016. *www .merriam-webster.com/dictionary/vet.*

CHAPTER 13

1. Boyle, Susan. "I Dreamed a Dream." Syco Music, 2009, compact disc.

2. Hamel, Gary, and Michele Zanini. "Excess Management Is Costing the U.S. $3 Trillion Per Year." *Harvard Business Review*, September 5, 2016. *https://hbr.org/2016/09/excess-management-is-costing-the-us -3-trillion-per-year.*

3. Havel, Vaclav. "The Need for Transcendence in the Postmodern World." Speech made in Independence Hall, Philadelphia, July 4, 1994. *www.worldtrans.org/whole/havelspeech.html.*

Index

A

Accountability, 56, 84–85, 87–88, 99, 142
Adaptability, 185
Agility, 10, 53, 185
Airbnb, 103
Alien, 163
Alsbury, Mike, 52
Ama OluKai Foundation, 105
Amazon, 72
American Financial Group, 136
Anderson, Rick, 31–32, 34–36, 45, 139
Anecdote, 167
Angie's Kettlecorn, 73
Anxiety, 60
Aphorism, 167
Appreciative inquiry, 186
Aristotle, 52, 164–165
Artifacts, 59
Assumptions
    disarming of, 140
    underlying, in organizational culture,
        60
Authenticity, 162

B

Baschera, Pius, 120, 122, 124, 130, 132,
    139
Basho, Matsuo, 165
Basic human needs, 5
Bastean, Todd, 76–80, 111
Behaviors
    accountability for, 87–88
    evolving nature of, 113
    by leaders, 81, 89, 140, 154
    role-modeling of, 89, 162
    work-related, 21
Beliefs, espoused, 59–60
Bezos, Jeff, 116
Bold, being, 51–52, 63–64, 69–70, 73, 196
Bolt, Jim, 17
Boomer generation, xiv
Boyle, Susan, 197
Brand
    building of, 105–106
    connectedness to, 105–107
    development of, 32–33
    My Health, My St. Luke's, 32, 34–35,
        37, 189
    organizational culture as foundation
        of, 33–34
    vision and, 44–46
Brand identity
    case studies of, 33–34, 42–43
    criteria for, 33
Brand initiative, 32–33
Brand strategy, 106
Branson, Richard, 52–53, 116
Brattle Bookstore, 163
Britain's Got Talent?, 197
Brown, Brené, 81
Bumble Bee Seafoods, 39–45, 51, 189
Bunge North America, 76–79, 81, 111
Bureaucracy, 197
Businesses, xvii. *See also* Organization(s)

C

CBridge Partners, 142
Chakrabarty, Prosanta, 164

Champion 2020, 124
Champion 3C, 122
Change
    compelling vision achieved through,
        148
    deciding for, 185–188
    failure of, 141
    lack of buy-in through the
        organization for, 140–147
    in organizations, 90
Charismatic leaders, 116
Charter, team, 89–91
Chouinard, Yvon, 17–18
Clarity
    as tool, 95–97
    before strategy, 92–95
    benefits of, 56
    case study of, 83–92
    of conversation, 97–98
    definition of, 85, 191
    in expectations, 87–88
    forging of, 54–56, 83–100, 191
    individual, 86
    job satisfaction and, 56
    lack of, 96
    levels of, 85–86
    need for, 197
    organizational, 85
    team, 85
    team charter, 89–91
    workgroup, 85
Coaching
    case studies of, 149–152
    team, 192–193
Cognitive readiness, 185
Collective vision, 44
Collins, Simon, 57
Columbia Business School, 176
Commitment
    belief in compelling vision and, 22
    employee, 87, 91
    by leader, 199
    organizational, 57
Communication
    effectiveness of, 188
    email, 171
    importance of, 148

oral, 170
organizational hierarchy effects on,
    142
of vision, 115
Communication sector, 65
Community
    need to belong to, 5
    sense of, 197–198
Compelling vision. *See also* Vision
    as visualization exercise, 21, 94
    benefits of, 10
    blueprint for, 181–193
    case studies of, 22–28, 72–75
    change necessary for achieving, 148
    by charismatic leaders, 116
    commitment created through belief
        in, 22
    companies built around, 116
    creation of, 12, 47, 114–116
    development of, 7–9, 47, 50
    elements of, 8
    emotion used to create, 158
    excitement generated by, 19
    for Generation Y, 15
    lack of buy-in through the
        organization for, 140–147, 183
    leadership techniques needed to
        create, 50
    personal connectedness with, 28. *See
        also* Connectedness
    personalizing of, 115–116
    power of, 20
    process for creating, 114–116
    productivity affected by, 22
    purpose of, 20
    scientific research regarding, 20
    staff turnover affected by, 22
Competition, 142–143
Connectedness. *See also* Connectivity
    with a compelling vision, 28
    to brand, 105–107
    building of, 56–57, 191
    components for, 38
    employee, 38, 56–57, 107–110, 113,
        162–163
    with Generation Y, 2–3, 13
    growth and profit benefits of, 111–112

in leading with vision, 45
loss of, 6
loyalty through, 11
money versus, 3, 5
organizational culture of, 113–114
resource allocation affected by, 21
sharing of vision as method of, 110
storyteller's power to create, 178
Connectivity. *See also* Connectedness
building of, 56–57, 101–117
emotional, 56, 102, 105, 115, 181
OluKai case study of, 103–111
Consequences, clarity of, 88
Contract, 184
Contradiction, 167
Conversations
clarity of, 97–98
T-shaped, 143
vision as basis for, 144
Coresystems, 64–72, 75, 81, 103
Cornell University, 73
Corporate bureaucracy, 197
Corporate vision, 12, 123–125, 143, 154
Courage
in boldness, 51–52, 63–64, 69–70, 73, 196
in decision making, 53
description of, 51
embodying of, 63–82, 189–191
leading with, 81
standing firm as, 54
vulnerability as, 52–54, 75–77
word origin of, 77
Cowell, Simon, 197
CPP, Inc., 101–102
Credibility
of leaders, 50, 81
of storytellers, 174
Crowdsourcing, of customer service, 66–67
Culture. *See also* Organizational culture
as competitive advantage, 132–133
definition of, 119
development of, 122–123
differing types of, 191
feedback-rich, 145–147

Hilti Corporation case study of, 120–133
importance of, 198
innovation and, 121–122, 125–126
investment in, 128–129
of storytelling, 179. *See also* Storytelling
training of, 127
vision and, 59, 133, 198
"Culture Eats Everything for Breakfast, Lunch and Dinner," 58, 119
Culture planning, 127–128, 130–133
Culture shaping, 58–59, 119–134, 191, 198
Culture unity, 138–139
Curtis, Alastair, 96
Customer service
barriers to, 66
case study of, 64–68
crowdsourcing of, 66–67
employee commitment effects on, 87
intelligent matching in, 72
poor, 65
real-time, 71
studies regarding, 65
in telecom industry, 70

D

Dancing with the St. Louis Stars, 80
Dead Poets Society, 159
Decision making
courage in, 53
emotion and, 158
Delaney, Pete, 22–28
Differentiation, 61
Disengagement of employees, 6
Disney, Walt, 52
Drucker, Peter, 119
Dual-leader setup, 136
Dubuque, Susan, 32–33

E

Eastman, George, 10
Einstein, Albert, 185
e-Literate, 176

Emails, 171
EMC, 143
Emotion(s)
    connecting with, 157–159
    engaging of employees through, 159,
        165
    power of, 160–161
    in vision, 56, 102, 161–162
Emotional connectivity, 56, 102, 105,
        115, 181
Empathy, 54
Employees
    in achieving of vision, 55
    belief in vision by, 8
    commitment by, 87, 91
    compelling vision's effect on, 21
    connectedness, 38, 56–57, 107–110,
        113, 162–163
    development of, 131
    disengagement of, 6
    emotional connectivity with, 102, 165
    empowering of, 36, 115, 145, 179
    engaging of, 87, 123, 130, 141, 159,
        165, 198
    excitement by, 18–19
    flexibility for, 126–127
    on-boarding of, 90–91
    supportive of, 163
    turnover of, 22, 110
    in vision creation, 144
    work-related behaviors of, 21
Empowerment
    feedback for fostering of, 145–147
    leadership's role in, 35–36
    prototyping process for, 115
    storytelling as method of, 179
    technology used for, 68
    vulnerability in, 53
Enable Midstream, 23
Endangered Species, 73
Espoused beliefs and values, 59–60
Ethics, 173
Executive coaching, 193
Executive development, 47–48
Executive Development Associates, xiii,
        7, 17, 184
Executive unity, 138–139

Expectations
    clarity of, 87–88, 162
    description of, xiii
    realistic, 87

F

Face-to-face meetings, 97
Family concept, 109
Family values, 110–111
Feedback, 98, 123, 128, 138, 145–148
Feely, Matthew, 177
Fields, Donna, 35, 37
Film, 176
Financial numbers
    as leaders' motivation, 22
    as vision, 12
    leading by, 4–5
Fitzgerald, Lucy, 80
Fleet management, 126
"Fog of war," 9
Followership, 88–89
Forward-looking, 50

G

GE, 139, 172
Generation X, xiv
Generation Y
    clarity levels and, 86
    compelling vision for, 15
    connecting with, 101
    description of, 1–3
    engagement with, 13, 142
    face-to-face conversations with, 99
    motivation of, xv, 13, 191
    needs of, 15
    personal connectedness with, 2–3,
        13
    transparency and, 174
    in workforce, xiv, 57, 102
Genuineness, 174
GMO, 73–74, 188
Goals
    accountability for, 87
    aligning of, 87
    clarity of, 55

communication to, 55
courage to set, 51
definition of, 28
focusing on, 163
measurability of, 88
self-assessments, 187
Greer, Lindred, 136
Grenacher, Manuel, 64–72, 75, 81
Grieco, Anthony, 181

H

Haiku, 165
Hamel, Gary, 197
Harris, Jim, 103–107, 110–111
Havel, Vaclav, 195–196
Health Food Business, 75
Hennessey, J. T., 59
Higher-order thinking skills, 185
Hilti, Eugen, 120
Hilti, Martin, 120, 126
Hilti, Michael, 129
Hilti Corporation, 120–133, 138, 192, 198
Hitler, Adolf, 160–161
Hubbard, Elbert, 163
Huffington, Arianna, 116
Hyde Space, 142–143
Hyperbole, 167

I

Imagery, 20, 108, 158, 167
In the Telling, 175, 178
Inc.com, 161
Individual clarity, 86
Information processing, 158
Innovation
    in asset management, 126
    culture and, 121–122, 125–126
    description of, 61
    encouraging of, 132
Innovation communities, 143–144
Insanity, 185
INSEAD business school, 96–97
Insigniam Quarterly, 58, 119
Integrity, 54, 95, 131, 173–174

Intelligent matching, 72
Invisible, imagining of, 182–183

J

Jimbo's, 72–75, 169, 188
Job satisfaction, 56
Jobs, Steve, 116
Johnson, Kevin, 175–176, 178
Johnson, Kristi Overton, 43–44, 94
Journal of Property Management, 57

K

Karaoke Capitalism, 61
KBS, 142
Keating, John, 159
Kennedy, John F., 171–172, 189, 196
KKR, 136
Kodak, 10–12, 22
KPMG U.K., 57

L

Lack of personal development by the
    leader, 148–153
Lack of unity, 135–139
Lack of urgency, 135, 147–148
Language, 167
Larsen, Jeff, 175
Leaders
    behaviors by, 81, 89, 140, 154
    challenges faced by, 195
    charismatic, 116
    commitment by, 199
    competencies needed by, 49
    courageous. *See* Courage
    credibility of, 50, 81
    empathy by, 54
    empowerment by, 36
    in fog, 8–10
    forward-looking by, 50
    impact of, on culture, 190
    lack of personal development by,
        148–153
    mistakes by, 36–37
    power struggles among, 136–138

Leaders (*Cont.*)
  qualities admired in, 50
  rhetorical devices used by, 167
  self-awareness by, 154–155
  self-improvement by, 150
  shifts by, xvi
  strengths of, 190
  visionary, 37–39, 97, 195
  vulnerability of, 52–54, 75–76, 80
  weaknesses of, 190
Leadership
  in culture shaping, 59
  empowerment from, 35–36
  retention of, 129–130
  transactional, 174–175
  transformational, 174–175
  visionary, 96–97, 195, 197
  in VUCA environment, 53
*Leadership Challenge: How to Make
    Extraordinary Things Happen in
    Organizations, The*, 50
Leadership development, 7, 129–130, 195
Leadership techniques
  clarity. *See* Clarity
  connectedness. *See* Connectedness
  courage. *See* Courage
  culture. *See* Culture
  description of, 50
Leading
  with courage, 81
  by numbers, 4–5
Learning through mistakes, 36–37
Lehigh Valley Health Network, 33
Lerner, Jennifer, 158
Let My People Go Surfing, 17
Liability
  intelligence as, 152
  strengths that become, 153–154
Lichtenwalner, Tom, 37
"LIFT6: Leadership to Inspire Future
    Talent," 181–189, 193
Lincoln, Abraham, 183
Lischewski, Chris, 39–45, 51
Litotes, 167
Lofaso, Chris, 83–92, 97
Loyalty, xiv, 7, 11, 57
Loyalty in Business, 163

M

Ma, Jack, 116
Martin, Bob, 32
Maslow, Abraham, 5
Matrix organizational structure, 6
McLuhan, Marshall, 177
Mental imagery, 20
Microsoft, 10, 12, 22, 85, 97
Mila, 68
Mind-set, 22–24, 111, 119, 122, 126, 136,
    178
Mission, 28
Mission statements, 121–122, 161
Mistakes, learning through, 36–37
Money, personal connectedness versus,
    3, 5
Morgan, Piers, 197
Motivation
  financial numbers as, 22
  of Generation Y, xv, 13
Musk, Elon, 116
Myers-Briggs Type Indicator®, 101–102

N

Narrative, 165
National Aeronautics and Space
    Administration, 189
Neathawk, Dubuque & Packett, 32
Negativity, 178
Net Promoter Score, 71
New York Public Library, 143–144
New Yorker, 96
Nokia, 96–97
Nooyi, Indra, 116
Nordström, Kjell, 61

O

Obstacles
  lack of buy-in through the
      organization, 140–147, 183
  lack of personal development by the
      leader, 148–153
  lack of unity, 135–139
  lack of urgency, 147–148

preconceived notions, 139–140
OGE Energy Corporation, 23–28, 169
OluKai, 103–111, 158, 169, 198
On-boarding of new employees, 90–91
ON!Track, 126
"Operation Tomodachi," 177
Options, creating of, 184–185
Oracle, 136
Organization(s)
  agility in, 53
  change in, 90
  communication in, 142
  compelling vision's effect on, 21
  culture of. *See* Culture;
      Organizational culture
  matrix structure of, 6
Organizational clarity, 85
Organizational commitment, 3, 22,
    56–57
Organizational culture
  artifacts, 59
  basic underlying assumptions, 60
  brand identity based on, 33–34
  changing of, 58
  connectedness in, 113–114
  definition of, 58
  espoused beliefs and values, 59–60
  feedback-rich, 145–147
  Hilti Corporation case study of,
    120–133
  importance of, 26
  leader's impact on, 190
  shaping of, 58–61
  at St. Luke's University and Health
      Network, 32
  underlying assumptions in, 60
  vision achievement affected by, 59, 133
Our Culture Journey, 127–128
Overton, Parker, 43

P

Paradox, 167
Passion, 162
Patagonia, 17–18, 184, 188
Personal connectedness.
      See Connectedness

Personal support, 193
Plato, 164, 170
Poetics, 165
Poetics, The, 164–165
Poetry, 159–160, 165–166
Popcorn Indiana, 73
Positivity, in storytelling, 178
Power of three, 166
Power struggles, 136–138
Preconceived notions, 139–140, 154
Presidents, 171–172
Private equity values, 110–111
Productivity, 22
Progress monitoring, 88
Prototyping, 115

R

Radicati, 171
Reagan, Ronald, 171–172
Real-time customer service, 72
Red Hat, 142, 184
Relationships, 12
Respect, 5, 90
Rhetoric, 166–167
Ridderstråle, Jonas, 61
Risk taking, 132
"Role of Emotions in Marketing, The," 158
Role-modeling of behaviors, 89, 162

S

Safety
  description of, 27–29
  vision for, 76–80
Schank, Roger, 170, 179
Self-awareness, 148, 154–155
Senior leadership, xv
Sense of direction, 9–10
Shared vision, i, 50, 76, 140, 142, 147
Short-term vision, 91
Slaaen, Eivind, 120, 122, 125, 128–130,
    139
Smithsonian, 164
Social validation, 60
Socrates, 170
Someck, Jim "Jimbo," 72–75, 81, 89

Speaking, 160–161
Spender, J.-C., 142
Sports, visualization in, 20, 43–44
St. Luke's University and Health
    Network, 31–35, 38, 45, 139
Staff turnover, 3, 22, 56, 110
Stand Up for Safety program, 78
Standing firm, 54
Stanford Graduate School of Business,
    136
Storytellers
    credibility of, 174
    description of, 169, 173
    enthusiasm of, 174
    integrity of, 173–174
    power of, 173
    self-assessment questions for, 175–176
    success as, 178–179
    transmedia, 175–178
Storytelling
    in ancient Greece, 165, 169–179
    definition of, 172
    description of, 169–171
    integrity in, 174
    mastery of, 171
    message delivery considerations in,
        177
    positivity in, 178
    by presidents, 171–172
    transactional leadership in, 174–175
    transformational leadership in,
        174–175
    at work, 172–173
*Strategic Conversations: Creating and
    Directing the Entrepreneurial
    Workforce*, 142
Strengths, 190
Stress, 14
Strong, Bruce A., 142, 144, 184
Success
    as storyteller, 178–179
    visualization of, 43–44
Sunfood Superfoods, 73
Surowiecki, James, 96
Sustainable value creation through
    leadership and differentiation,
    122–123

Swift, Jonathan, 183
Swisscom Friends, 68–69, 71

T

Team building, 41–42, 109
Team charter, 89–91
Team clarity, 85
Team coaching, 192–193
Team unity, 138–139
TED conferences, 164
*Tell Me a Story: Narrative and
    Intelligence*, 170, 179
Themes, 166
"Three-act script," 165
Time lines, 147–148
Transactional leadership, 174–175
Transformational leadership, 174–175
Transmedia storytellers, 175–178
Transparency, 174
Trends in Executive Development survey,
    xiii–xiv, 7, 46–48, 185
Trust, 81, 84, 173–174
T-shaped conversations, 143
Turtle Island, 73

U

Uber, 67, 103
Underlying assumptions, in
    organizational culture, 60
Understanding, fostering of, 189
Understanding Media, 177
United States Federal Civil Service, 59
Unity
    culture, 138–139
    executive, 138–139
    lack of, 135–139
    team, 138–139
Urgency, lack of, 135, 147–148

V

Values
    alignment of, 130
    espoused, 59–60
    family, 110–111

at Hilti Corporation, 131
private equity, 110–111
sustainable creation of, through
    leadership and differentiation,
    122–123
Vetting of vision, 183–184
Virgin Galactic, 52, 55
Vision. *See also* Compelling vision
    alignment with, 145
    boldness in, 51–52, 63–64, 69–70, 73
    brand and, 44–46
    by charismatic leaders, 116
    clarity of, 8, 54–55, 196–197
    collective, 44
    communication of, 55, 115
    connectedness through sharing of,
        110
    conveying of, 162
    corporate, 12, 123–125, 143, 154
    creation of, 142
    culture and, 59, 198
    definition of, 20, 28
    development of, xiv–xv
    dream for, 115
    emotional connection with, 56, 102,
        161–162
    employee involvement in, 144
    employees' belief in, 8
    financial numbers as focus of, 12
    goal of, 7
    lack of buy-in through the
        organization for, 140–147, 183
    personalizing of, 115–116
    presenting of, 163–164
    purpose of, 20
    for safety, 76–80
    shared, i, 50, 76, 140, 142, 147
    sharing of, 163
    short-term, 91
    transformation through, 141

vetting of, 183–184
visual image of, 7–8, 44
workforce's involvement in, 144
Vision statements, 10–11, 72, 161
Visionary leaders, 37–39, 97, 195
Visionary leadership, 96–97, 195, 197
Visualization
    compelling vision creation through,
        21, 44, 94
    power of, 20
    sharing of, 162
    in sports, 20, 43–44
    of success, 43–44
VUCA environment, 9, 53, 196
Vulnerability, 52–54, 75–77, 80–81, 151,
    162

W

Weaknesses
    description of, 190, 199
    vulnerability versus, 76, 81
Welch, Jack, 139
Whole Foods, 136
Whole Foods, 75
Williams, Robin, 159
Wisdom of Crowds, The, 96
Workforce
    authenticity and, 113–114
    Generation X in, xiv
    Generation Y in, xiv, 57, 102
Workgroup clarity, 85
Work-related behaviors, 21
Writing, 165–166
Wurman, Richard Saul, 164

Z

Zanini, Michele, 197

About the Authors

BONNIE HAGEMANN is CEO of Executive Development Associates, a boutique consulting firm specializing in top-of-the-house executive development and development of high potentials into senior leaders.

JOHN MAKETA is Chief Revenue Officer at Caliper. He is a strategy advisor who works with companies to develop skills for next generation leaders.

SIMON VETTER is CEO of StandOut International. He is a dynamic speaker, trainer, and coach for top companies around the world, including Microsoft, Toyota, Siemens, UBS, and more.